MASTERPIECES OF
ARCHITECTURAL DRAWING

MASTERPIECES OF ARCHITECTURAL DRAWING

EDITED BY HELEN POWELL AND DAVID LEATHERBARROW

ABBEVILLE PRESS. PUBLISHERS. NEW YORK

Title page: A drawing by Joseph Gandy, dated 1836, showing many different styles of architecture all in one building, and sometimes called Comparative Styles of Architecture or The Mythological House. (John Soane's Museum, London)

Copyright © 1982 Orbis Publishing Ltd.

First published in the USA 1983 by
Abbeville Press Inc
505 Park Avenue
New York
New York 10022

ISBN 0-89659-326-6

Published simultaneously in the United Kingdom by Orbis Publishing Ltd and in Canada by Hurtig Publishers Ltd.

Printed and bound in the Netherlands

CONTENTS

LIST OF PLATES

PREFACE

An introductory history of architectural drawing is a deceptively simple idea, but the subject covers a curiously elusive area of study which cuts across many different historical and aesthetic disciplines. The difficulty of such a survey may be judged by the fact that the last time such a book appeared was in 1912, when the Edwardian architect and writer Sir Reginald Blomfield published his own history of architectural drawing, *Architectural Drawing and Draughtsmen.* He wrote as an enthusiast, and his particular interest in the French Renaissance resulted in a book with a very distinct bias which would not be acceptable in a general survey made today.

In order to achieve as balanced a discussion as possible, this book has been assembled from the advice and help of a number of people. What they have said and written has been woven together to form the text and picture selection which follows. The original idea for the book came from Alexandra Artley, who felt that an historical survey of architectural drawing would be of immense interest to people who have no specialist background in the subject. For contributions and expert revisions to the text the editors are indebted to Alan Powers, John Martin Robinson and Gavin Stamp. Louis Dezart prepared the drawings and explanations of technical terms which appear in the glossary, Alan Powers supplied the short note on materials and lettering, and the bibliography has been compiled by the editors. Thanks are due to Annabel Davies and Sarah Coombe for invaluable assistance with picture research and to Mary Evans for painstaking design work. Those who contributed to the notes, in addition to the editors, are as follows: Peter Carl, Catherine Harding, James Macaulay, Alan Powers, John Martin Robinson, Gavin Stamp, David Walker and Dalibor Vesely.

This perspective, of the Principal Staircase of the Palace of a Sovereign by Emmanuel Brune, was one of a group of drawings which won the *1er Grand Prix* of the École des Beaux Arts in 1863. For a section of this same project see Plate 62 on pages 130-1.

INTRODUCTION

The art of Drawing . . . may justly be called a bearing Mother of all Arts and Sciences whatever, for whatsoever is made begets thorow {through} the same a good Aspect and well-being; and besides all this, the Art of Drawing is the Beginning and End, or Finisher of all things imaginable, wherefore she may be called a Sense of Poesie, a Second Nature, a Living Book of all things . . .

Gerhard of Brugge: *An Introduction to the General Art of Drawing,* 1674.

The architectural drawings that can be called masterpieces are, like the buildings they represent, both useful and beautiful. They aid builders and can be studied as works of art. Moreover, they can convey a range of beliefs and an array of practices. Often they depict the workings of the architect's imagination. At other times they are made to seduce clients or the judges of a competition. They have a range of functions and this is what differentiates them from the diagrams of an engineer and the drawings of a painter. In recent times it has become common to divide architectural drawings into two distinct types: the construction drawing and the presentation drawing. But this is an artificial division. The primary function of the architectural drawing is to provide information for builders in a form that symbolizes cultural values. Through time, a wide variety of types and techniques of drawings has emerged, and it is the intention of this book to introduce this rich and diverse subject to the layman.

Examples of drawings from the Middle Ages to the present have been selected to illustrate the history of architectural drawing as a form of art in its own right. In doing this it is hard to be entirely consistent as many artists have drawn buildings without practising architecture, and some architects, like Piranesi, have built little but greatly affected the way in which subsequent generations looked at buildings. It would need a far longer book to describe all the changes which have occurred in architectural drawing, and many of these changes only concern the development of office practice and 'working' drawings. This book draws mainly on examples of architects' design drawings or drawings which show the design of buildings in a non-technical way. It will be evident that many great architects are not represented. This is partly due to constrictions of space and partly due to the fact that not all great architects produce interesting drawings. The most lavish drawings were made during the nineteenth and early twentieth century. It was the first period during which architects devoted a great deal of effort to making beautiful, highly finished drawings which were intelligible to the lay public.

These 'presentation' drawings were often produced for exhibition or reproduction so their public appeal was carefully considered. Nevertheless, architectural drawings from a variety of periods can be of equal interest and beauty to modern eyes.

In defining architectural drawing a strict frame of reference would only include drawings done before the construction of a building. While examples which are most obviously topographical are excluded, it is not always possible to be certain whether drawings were done before or after building construction. In many cases designs were often made for unrealizable buildings either because they depicted 'fantastic' architecture or because the building was just not built. Such drawings, however, often played a profound role in the development of architectural ideas and in their techniques of representation. A strict definition might also confine the choice to works which were 'autograph' drawings, excluding prints and engravings. However, architectural drawing has been so closely bound up with the processes of graphic reproduction that this definition would leave out much valuable material from periods when artists of all kinds made prints as a natural way of circulating their ideas. Lastly, architects have often copied each other's drawings in order to learn techniques of draughtmanship or to record the information contained in the drawing. This practice was especially prevalent during the Renaissance when sketchbooks formed the basis of the architect's training. From about 1500 onwards architects also began systematically to reproduce antique remains and contemporary buildings through sketches and measured drawings. Although strictly topographical by definition, these drawings also form part of the fabric of architectural ideas; it was the architect's way of 'drawing from life'.

There is obviously a great deal more to architectural drawing than could be covered in this book, but it is hoped that the examples presented here will show that when architects put pen or pencil to paper in order to pass their ideas on to others, the mastery of the means of communication may not be unrelated to the nature and quality of the ideas in question. The relationship between an architect's thinking, drawing and seeing is highly complex, possibly because it links together these fundamental human activities. Nevertheless, it is clear that drawings are more than a graphic expression of ideas: architects think and imagine by drawing. It is hoped that this book will provide an interesting introduction to the subject for anyone discovering the delights of studying and collecting architectural drawings for the first time.

THE HISTORY OF ARCHITECTURAL DRAWING

In tracing how drawings have changed throughout history, those of Antiquity have by and large been omitted and examples taken from the 'Western' tradition since the late Middle Ages. Again, this is partly due to the pressure of space but it is also due to the fact that the historical sequence chosen has a homogeneity which forms the tradition of architectural drawing as we still understand it.

Medieval Drawing

From the Middle Ages, the period bridging late Antiquity and the emergence of the modern world, approximately 2000 architectural drawings have survived. One factor crucial to the understanding of these drawings is that the builders of the time were far more capable than we are today of thinking out large structures in three dimensions, and much medieval building, particularly of cathedrals, was based on geometrical calculations for which drawings were unnecessary. The question of what medieval scholars and masons themselves meant by 'theoretical' as opposed to 'practical' geometry is itself a complex academic problem which lies beyond the scope of this book, although pointers to further reading are given in the Bibliography.

In the early Middle Ages drawings were not used by the builder to help him solve any technical problems before work began. Details of a building tended to be drawn (one function of a master mason, for example, was to provide full-scale templates for the mouldings of piers and arches) but plans and elevations of the entire project were not drawn. There is minimal evidence that elaborate plans were drawn for Gothic cathedrals. Very few pre-thirteenth-century plans have survived. It may be that few were drawn. More probably, the materials onto which they were drawn – parchment, wooden planks or sheets of fresh plaster – were exceedingly fragile. In addition, masons saw no reason to preserve drawings after their buildings were completed. The palimpsest represents another problem: many drawings which were executed on parchment were eradicated so that the sheet could be (repeatedly) reused. Whether or not drawings were used, full-scale ground plans were laid out on the ground using stakes, cords and simple instruments. The presence of the master builder was therefore indispensable to the construction of the building, and this accounts for the fact that some masters were bound by contract to remain in the area until their work was done. Gervase of Canterbury records that when William of Sens (*fl.* 1174-80) was injured by a fall from the scaffolding of

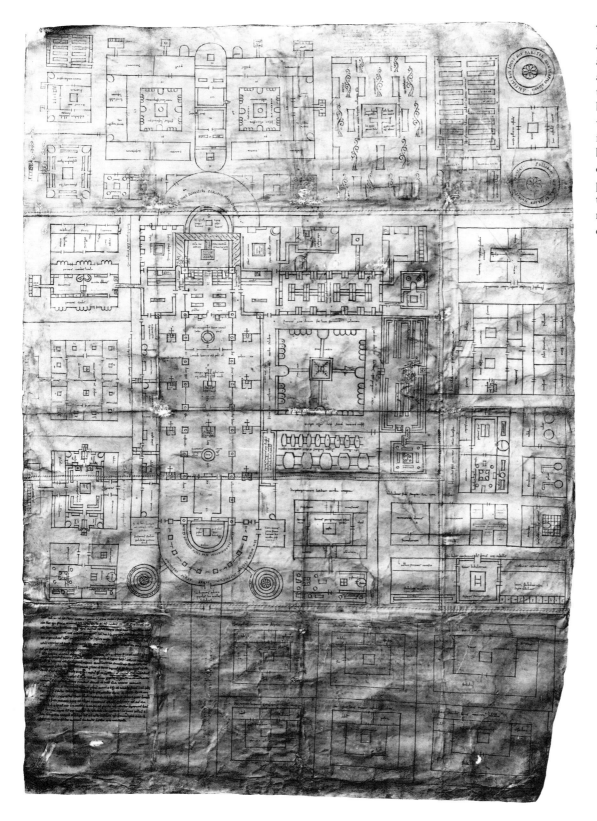

This plan of St Gall, Switzerland (pen and ink on parchment), drawn in about 820 AD, is the only surviving architectural drawing before the twelfth century. It shows a group of buildings for living, work and prayer, with the church, the largest building, in the centre, serving the needs of both monks and pilgrims to the tomb of St Gallus. The plan gives a detailed picture of what was then regarded as the ideal Benedictine monastery, never built but setting a standard for others to emulate.

the choir of Canterbury Cathedral in 1179, he continued to direct operations from his bed, commanding 'what work must be done first and what {work} afterwards'.

The tracing-house or 'lodge' where projects were drawn and preserved is first mentioned in an English text in 1274 and some scholars feel that later medieval project drawings (i.e. drawings made before the building is built) emerged from the traditional use of full-scale drawings of parts. The oldest extant project drawings are those in the Reims palimpsest made in or near the Reims area between 1240 and 1260. Certainly by the late medieval period drawings for façades and details exist which do seem to have been intended as projects for buildings.

Apart from the celebrated plan of S. Gall dating from *circa* 820 AD, an idealized drawing for a monastery which was never built, the body of medieval architectural drawings with which non-specialists are most familiar comprises those drawn after the event, i.e. drawings in which an observer noted down for future reference the solution to a particular problem or a particularly effective design. This category includes, for example, all the drawings in the celebrated notebook of Villard d'Honnecourt. Villard, an architect who was born at Honnecourt in Picardy in the first half of the thirteenth century, compiled a sketchbook *circa* 1235 which is now preserved in the Bibliothèque Nationale in Paris. Small in size, it is a fragment of thirty-three folios with approximately 325 drawings. During the course of his working life Villard travelled to Switzerland and Hungary, and the places he visited—Vaucelle, Cambrai, Meaux, Laon, Reims, Chartres and Lausanne—are recorded in drawings with accompanying explanatory notes. He demonstrated how to construct ground plans and elevations of Gothic buildings and sketched architectural ornaments, church furniture and mechanical devices, as well as human and animal bodies. Part sketchbook and part pattern book, the existence of this and presumably other similar books helps to account for the rapid dissemination of Gothic forms throughout Europe. The wide range of subjects illustrated in the book—details, decoration, proportional

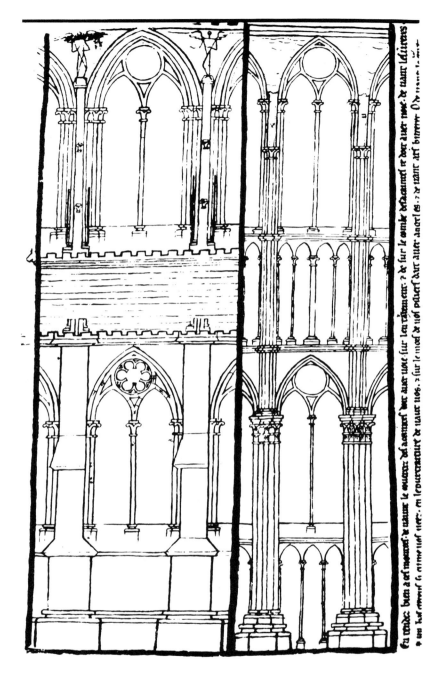

This page from the notebook of Villard d'Honnecourt shows a Reims choir chapel, inside and out. The mobility of masons during the Middle Ages is demonstrated by d'Honnecourt's notebook, which is a unique survival of a mason's commonplace book. Villard recorded details that interested him on buildings he visited during the 1220s, most notably the plan of Cambrai Cathedral, the oxen on the towers at Laon, and the new window tracery of Reims, shown here.

systems, geometrical diagrams and sculptural figures– suggests that the book served as a memory aid, instruction manual and source of design ideas. Drawn in ink on vellum with a spirited and strong line, this little volume provides us with a unique glimpse into the work of an enquiring and enthusiastic High Gothic mind.

Another medieval book containing interesting architectural drawings is the *Buchlein von der Fialen Gerechtigkeit,* or *Booklet on the Correct Design of Pinnacles,* published by the south German master mason, Matthias Roriczer in 1486 and dedicated to Wilhelm von Reichenau, Bishop of Eichstätt. During the course of his working life Roriczer held positions at Eichstätt, Nürnberg, Munich and Regensburg and a few years later he also published a twelve-page booklet called *Geometrica deutsch* on the application of geometry to building. In the design of pinnacles Roriczer drew on the design techniques of the Parler family of fourteenth-century master masons from Prague and this fascinating booklet is now kept in the Universitätsbibliothek at Würzburg.

Hans Schmuttermayer, a master mason from Nürnberg and a contemporary of Matthias Roriczer, also wrote a book concerned with the design of pinnacles. Schmuttermayer's *Fialenbüchlein* is clearly illustrated and an example of his architectural rendering of a pinnacle and gable is given on page 63. His drawings are less well known than those of Roriczer, but are considered by medieval scholars to be of special interest as they reveal how medieval master masons manipulated geometrical forms to develop their own individual architectural designs.

The late medieval–early Renaissance paintings of Cimabue (1240-1302), Duccio (1260-1340), Giotto (1267-1336) and Masaccio (1401-28) provide a key to the transformation of architectural drawing in Italy in the fourteenth and early fifteenth centuries. Whereas high Gothic art represented cities and buildings as flat, outline figures, the images of these painters introduced depth and foreshortening into their architectural scenes. There was a continuous tradition of non-mathematical perspective throughout the medieval period, stemming from the art of Antiquity and Byzantium. But the workshop practice of the middle centuries was transformed in the studios of Giotto and Masaccio. In fact, architectural drawings have been attributed to Giotto, who was an architect and a painter. The new spatial designs of Brunelleschi, Alberti and Piero della Francesca were based upon a tradition of pictorial representation that existed, in varying degrees of intensity, from ancient times.

The Italian Renaissance and Perspective Theory

Leone Battista Alberti (1404-72) was the first to codify the system of one-point perspective in a written treatise. He probably derived his system from Brunelleschi (1377-1446) who carried out practical experiments in setting up perspective 'views' using peepholes and mirrors. His architecture contained a lucid perspectival quality similar to the painted architecture of Giotto. However, the theory of Alberti's perspective system also drew heavily on the sciences of medieval optics and Classical geometry. Alberti published his perspective system in *Della Pittura,* which was written for painters and set forth the first modern theory of painting. It grounded art in visual experience and its 'geometric' representation. In his treatise on architecture, *De re aedificatoria,* which was the first architectural treatise of the Renaissance to crystallize current ideas on proportion, the orders, and town planning, he advised architects against using perspective drawings. Instead he recommended the traditional techniques of design: the ground plan and the model. For Alberti the ground plan contained the key proportions and principal measurements of the building. For example, all the heights of the elements of the building were determined by the proportions contained in the ground plan. The model demonstrated the three-dimensional appearance of the building and because it was true to scale, it could function as a 'working drawing' for the builder. In the actual practice of early Renaissance building a decision on the design of the building would be reached by the client on the evidence of the plan and verbal descriptions by the architect. This procedure was followed until the end of the fifteenth century. Leonardo and Bramante were perhaps the first systematically to use different modes of design in architecture to that recommended by Alberti.

Leonardo da Vinci (1452-1519) was fascinated by the problems and potentials of perspective construction. During the first years of his research into perspective he accepted Alberti's system. However, the results of his various studies led him to become disillusioned with the 'harmonic boxes' which were the outcome of this system. The method of projecting the delineations of objects onto a plane, as if it were 'transparent glass' like a 'window', did not correlate with Leonardo's demand for optical realism in representation. For example, Alberti's system could not deal with the curvature of straight lines as seen at the periphery of the visual field; nor could it regulate the apparent softening and blurring of form and colour seen as objects grew more distant. The other problem with 'window' perspective was that it set particular limits on the kind of information that could be shown. The 'window' or painter's perspective could only depict architecture by distorting the 'true' measurements and proportions and it could only represent that part of the building which could be seen in one glance. Though Leonardo never bequeathed to posterity a regular system of curvilinear or aerial perspective he introduced into architectural drawings, along with Bramante, the 'design' perspective in the form of the bird's-eye view (see Plate 8).

This convention developed out of his anatomical studies, in which he sought to explore the integrated 'mechanism' of the body. From a high vantage point one could gain a complete picture of an object as an entity and so convey the maximum of three-dimensional information. During the Renaissance the human body and the building were thought to be analogous, so the transference of this perspectival technique, from the study of anatomy to the design of building, was appropriate. In architectural design the bird's-eye view could elucidate the structural organization of volume and space; it could give complex information about the building's three-dimensional form; and it could help produce an idea of architecture that rejected the traditional distinction between 'design' (on one plane) and 'structure' (in three dimensions).

The bird's-eye view of a building had the facility of representing it as if it were a discrete, dynamically integrated organism. But the high and distant vantage point necessary to such a construction meant that there was no inherent sense of scale. This scale could only be intimated if the 'vanishing point' of the perspective construction was at eye level and if human figures formed part of the picture. The bird's-eye view had the advantage of minimizing distortion but it entailed a level of abstraction. In this way it is comparable to the modern 'axonometric'. During the Renaissance this type of drawing was limited to the design of buildings, rather than their execution, as they could not provide the builder with accurate dimensions. As a design aid, however, it gave the architect a new freedom to explore his ideas and a new technique by which he could control the design of the building.

Donato Bramante (1444-1514) was a key figure in the Renaissance innovation of perspective design in architecture. With his type of 'illusionistic' architecture the cautions of Alberti became irrelevant. The early Renaissance architects, following the medieval precedent in a classical guise, were concerned with the 'true' measurements of a building and had no need of the perspective sketch to act as an aid to their design. However, with Bramante, who was trained as a painter and was a friend of Leonardo, a change occurred. To him the methods of the painter and those of the architect were interchangeable. He was concerned with 'true' measurement, harmonic proportions and so forth, but he also conceived architecture as a 'picture': essentially, architecture became 'painting', a visual fact, a representation complete in itself. Unlike Brunelleschi, Bramante created 'illusions' of perspective to fill out the ideal appearance of the building. The famous example of this is his building of a false choir in the church of S. Maria presso S. Satiro. Illusionistic perspectives were much more subtle in his later works but the new conception of architecture which he inaugurated had a profound influence on architectural drawing. The desire to create, or recreate, the *effects* of Antique architecture, and the desire to elevate the status of the architect to that of the single creator of the building, combined in Bramante to produce a technique of sketching which at once recorded *views* of antique remains and his own *invenzione*. He gave new impetus to the development of both of these types of sketches (see Plate 7).

Bramante and his circle also used the bird's-eye perspective drawing to record ancient buildings and their own designs. This technique particularly suited the representation of centralized buildings and allowed their interiors to be represented by dissecting the building and drawing the section in perspective. In these drawings the section line corresponded to the plane of the paper, thus giving the impression that the interior was to be seen through a 'transparent glass' plane. Hence, in Alberti's terms, the interior was visualized as if it were a 'picture'. The drawback of this convention was that it only suited the depiction of plain, centralized interiors which the eye could take in at a glance, such as the Pantheon in Rome. In the representation of complex longitudinal interiors the spaces appeared to overlap. The bird's-eye sectional perspective best represented simple volumetric interiors where the emphasis was on the 'body' of the space, rather than the articulation of the walls.

In view of these observations, one would expect to find evidence of perspective sections in the drawings produced for the design of St Peter's, which Bramante intended to be the ultimate in centralized planning. However, such drawings were not produced. Instead the perspective section was used in another way and finally replaced by a method that rendered the interior in a basically different manner. The evolution of drawing techniques was reflected in the drawings made and collected by Giuliano da Sangallo (1445-1516) over several decades. In his views of Antique centralized buildings, he depicted the wall facing the viewer as if it were broken, in order to provide a partial view of the interior. He represented the spatial appearance of the building. In his later drawings, however, there is a tendency to revert to orthogonal projec-

tion, which is not capable of conveying spatial characteristics in the same way.

The probable originator of this change in technique was the great Classicist Raphael (1483-1520). He succeeded Bramante as chief architect in charge of the building of St Peter's and was faced with the complex task of continuing and adapting his predecessor's design, for which there was no clear and detailed set of intentions. In a famous letter to Pope Leo X, which concerned the representation of ancient Rome in drawings, Raphael insisted that architectural drawings should consist of the separate ground plan, elevation and section. His method entailed the abandonment of central perspective as used by Bramante and his pictoral 'views' of architecture. Raphael's systematic attempt to separate the different representations of architecture, and his abandonment of drawings which posited a single vantage point for the viewer, meant that the viewer of the building was intended to experience the space in a different way. For example, in Raphael's Chigi Chapel in Santa Maria del Popolo, the interior cannot be taken in at a single glance as Bramante's choir in the same church can be. In the Chigi Chapel the visitor has to gather together the culminative effect of many impressions, many glances. In a sense the change of 'viewpoint' can best be described as a change in perspective, for Bramante's 'picture' architecture was contrived around a distant viewpoint whilst Raphael designed his architecture from *inside* the space. His drawing of the interior of the Pantheon (Plate 13) demonstrates this idea; at the time of its execution it was considered a masterpiece of applied perspective. In this drawing the vantage point was assumed to lie approximately in the centre of the room and as the space was circular the perspective could not be drawn according to Alberti's precepts, that is, as if seen through a 'window'. Raphael's drawing did not represent the information gained from one fixed glance but a kind of 'multiple' perspective. As such it was halfway to being an orthogonal drawing and closer to what we might see through a wide-angle lens. The flattening effect allowed detail of the wall surfaces and the decoration to be shown more clearly. The

The drawing shown here is one of Giuliano Sangallo's many studies for St Peter's. What is unique about it is that it uses orthogonal represent-ation together with independent perspective constructions. The pilasters, engaged columns and niches are drawn as outlines on a flat plane, while the disengaged columns, vaults and side-chapel are shown in perspective. In fact, the three groups of clerestory windows are drawn with different vanishing points. Because the floor, ceiling and side walls are not shown, the drawing represents less than a constructed one-point perspective would have

shown, but because the independent perspectives give spatial depth, the drawing shows more than an orthogonal one would.

During his career Sangallo travelled all over Italy, studying ancient monuments and early *quattrocento* buildings. In 1513 Pope Leo X called him to Rome to assist Bramante in the *Fabbrica di S. Pietro*. When Bramate died a year later the team of successors – Sangallo, Fra Giocondo, Peruzzi and Raphael – was faced with the task of interpreting Bramante's intentions (without a plan) and modifying the over-ambitious design for the dome.

selection of the central, rather than distant, vantage point allowed the viewer of the drawing to imagine the space as a three-dimensional entity which included him. The sectional perspectives, on the other hand, confronted the viewer with an imaginery picture of the entire bisected space.

The studies by Peruzzi (1481-1536) and Giuliano da Sangallo for St Peter's show the same plurality of vantage points. In the so-called ideal view of St Peter's by Peruzzi the technique is paralleled by the combination of elements of the ground plan, elevation and section. The ground plan is drawn in perspective whilst the elevation is drawn 'as seen'. This complex and beautiful drawing did not make the separation between the three views recommended by Raphael. Although it gave an impression of spatiality it did not represent the appearance of the interior, nor did it supply the accurate measurements of the building. However, it did represent the organic connection between ground plan, exterior and interior in line with Leonardo's experimental drawings.

Peruzzi was reluctant to abandon the more visual practice of drawing in perspective for orthogonal projection which forced the artist and the viewer to accept multiple abstractions. It was probably Raphael's youngest colleague at St Peter's, Antonio da Sangallo the younger (1485-1546), who made the first consistent attempt to follow his precepts. He was the only great Renaissance architect from Rome who rose to the rank of architect from the building crafts as opposed to the painter's or sculptor's workshop. He was probably more sympathetic than Peruzzi to the 'professional' advantages of Raphael's system: the greater clarity and readability of the drawings and the advantages of being able to communicate design intentions accurately to a supervising architect. Bramante had managed to supervise building work himself but Raphael, as he had numerous other commissions, needed to devise a system that would ensure the continuance of the work if he was absent. Sangallo the younger became chief architect to St Peter's on the death of Raphael. The orthogonal projection became more generally known through the engravings of his pupil, Antonio Labacco, who reproduced Sangallo's designs for St Peter's by way of section and elevation. Later, Palladio, in his *Quattro Libri,* established the orthogonal view as the more professional representation indispensable for the realization of the actual building. Peruzzi's perspective constructions were popularized through Serlio's *Treatise* and were taken up by Androuet Du Cerceau and Fischer von Erlach, among others. This technique came to be known as 'cavalier projection' since it was concerned with picture-like visualization rather than accurate measurement.

The two methods of orthogonal and perspective representations were often used side by side until the end of the eighteenth century. From the example of Raphael it can be seen that the use of orthogonal projection did not necessarily

Peruzzi's sketch of the interior of S. Bernadino, Urbino, is set up as a single-point perspective. Unlike perspectives which place the vanishing point on an axis running in a perpendicular direction from the centre of the frontal plane, this drawing focuses on a corner in the depth of the space, giving a greater sense of spatial enclosure. Peruzzi was less interested in the quantifiable dimensions of metric space than the concrete qualities of inhabited space. He was a painter and designer of stage scenery as well as an architect, and he did not see painting and architecture as mutually exclusive or unrelated disciplines, but rather he saw them as complementary and overlapping.

entail an abandonment of perspective aesthetics in building. Arguments raged over whether perspective should be used to depict buildings and not over the accepted fact that buildings were seen in perspective. With illusionistic architecture this situation is apparent but it applied, nevertheless, to more mathematically 'correct' architecture as well. From their beginning perspective theories had a profound correspondence with the laws of optics and geometry and with the theories of proportion and number. Added to this there was a symbolic significance in the relationship between the viewer and the viewed which was embodied in perspective constructions. One example of this can be seen in Vignola's prejudice for central perspective which illogically coloured his technically correct description of two-point perspective in *Le due regole*

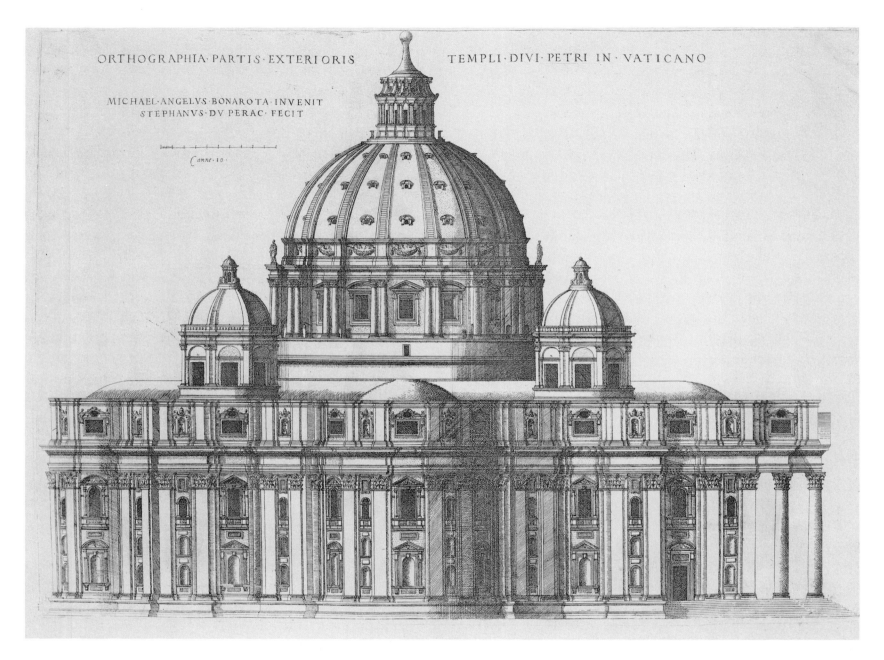

ORTHOGRAPHIA · PARTIS · EXTERIORIS   TEMPLI · DIVI · PETRI IN · VATICANO

MICHAEL · ANGELVS · BONAROTA · INVENIT
STEPHANVS · DV PERAC · FECIT

Canne · 10 ·

When Michelangelo succeeded Giuliano da Sangallo as architect-in-chief of St Peters, he shocked the administrators of the *Fabbrica* with two models which differed greatly from Sangallo's design. With the Pope's support, however, Michelangelo had his scheme accepted and, after refusing to take any payment, proceeded without interruption from meddling officials. This view of St Peter's was one of three engravings produced by Etienne Dupérac in 1569, five years after the death of Michelangelo. Dupérac's engravings, from models by Michelangelo, are the best records of the architect's intentions.

della prospettiva pratica . . ., published posthumously in 1583. Although there is no real difference between the two 'vanishing points' of the latter construction, Vignola insisted on the primacy of one of the points as a corresponding point to the eye. It was called the 'counter eye'. His treatise was probably the first in Italy to deal only with perspective construction. It was systematic and usable in form and its influence extended right up until the eighteenth century; by 1750 ten editions had been printed throughout Europe. It demonstrated a particular relationship between the viewer and the viewed. A similar prejudice can be found in the theory of shadow projections. Until the eighteenth century, shadows were always drawn as if they were cast from a point source of light. This light source was taken as being located on, or close to, the page of the drawing, even if the light source was supposed to be the sun. It was as if light was imagined as coming from an 'eye' which was located within the perspective construction. Such prejudices would seem to suggest that although Renaissance drawings appeared less like 'perspectives' than more recent applications of the technique, there was a deep connection between perspectivity and architecture.

Michelangelo Buonarroti (1475-1564) was one of the greatest and most influential of all architects, as well as a sculptor, painter and poet. He rejected all the assumptions of the Renaissance and revolutionized the vocabulary of architecture. His drawings reveal an entirely new approach to space in buildings, which he conceived as living structures. He preferred to make clay models of proposed buildings rather than perspective drawings, and seems not to have favoured the type of highly finished design from which builders could readily execute a work, but continuously modified his plans while work was in progress. His most important commission in Rome, where he spent the last part of his life, was for the completion of St Peter's, which was in fact still unfinished at the time of his death. He used detail drawings and elaborate models for his work on St Peter's, many of the details being modelled full-size in timber. For the dome of St Peter's, a clay model was followed by the famous wooden one which took over two years to make. (The best 'elevation' drawings for Michelangelo's scheme for St Peter's were made by Etienne Dupérac from the 1547 model and the 1558-61 dome model.) Michelangelo, however, occupies a unique place in the history of drawing. Giorgio Vasari (1511-74), the biographer, architect and painter, claimed that Michelangelo deliberately destroyed many of his drawings in order to conceal the amount of effort that he put into the development of every artistic project. On the other hand, Michelangelo was perhaps the first artistic 'celebrity' to be pressed for drawings by admirers who wanted them as keepsakes, and during his lifetime the idea we now take for granted—that drawings can be collected as independent works of art—emerged as a new notion of connoisseurship. It has been said that Vasari himself was the first collector of drawings for their own sake and that while preparing his *Lives of the Most Excellent Painters, Sculptors and Architects* (1550 and 1568) he conceived the revolutionary idea of collecting sample drawings from as many biographical subjects as possible in order to provide a visual record of their manner of working. From this period, drawings of all kinds became invaluable to collectors because, in the words of Goethe, 'they give in its purity the mental intention of the artist, . . . they bring immediately before us the mood of his mind at the moment of creation'.

For sensitive and historically invaluable drawings of ancient and modern buildings and sculpture in Rome during the period of Michelangelo's supremacy, the Italian sketchbooks of the Dutch painter Marten van Heemskerck (1498-1574) are an unrivalled record. At the end of the second decade of the fifteenth century, with the re-establishment of orthogonal drawing under Antonio da Sangallo the younger, there was also an increasing separation between professional architects and other artists, although this separation was never absolute until the nineteenth century. Perspective or 'semi-perspective' drawings continued in use together with orthogonal drawings for similar purposes in the work of Jacques Androuet Du Cerceau and Fischer von Erlach.

Andrea Palladio (1508-80), who has been called 'the first professional architect', established the primacy of orthogonal projections by confining the illustrations in his enormously influential *I Quattro Libri dell'Architettura* (1570) to plans, elevations and sections. Later, even the complex spatial conceptions of Francesco Borromini were actually put on paper in this way, unlike those of his contemporary and rival Bernini who had had a general artistic training.

Sixteenth-Century Publications

Printed architectural drawings fall into several categories. They may be records of work by an architect, records of ancient buildings, or reconstructions of buildings which may or may not have existed in such a form at some time. They may be illustrations to a treatise, or publications undertaken with the principal aim of self-advertisement.

The publications of the sixteenth century were mainly wood-cuts (cut with a knife and gouges on side-grain wood) and their quality varies, often within the same book, according to the skill of the engravers. The first notable illustrated book of architectural works was Francesco Colonna's *Hypneroto-machia Poliphili,* published in Venice in 1499, a dream fantasy which includes imaginary but precisely drawn interpretative reconstructions of ancient architecture among much other matter. The illustrations show interesting architectural forms such as a pyramid and an elephant carrying an obelisk on its back, and the figure drawing is of exceptionally high quality. The fact that the architectural drawings are accompanied by a number of emblematic and hieroglyphic figures is an indication of the symbolic character of the buildings represented in the book.

On a more strictly architectural level, the first practical illustrated treatise on architecture was Sebastiano Serlio's *L'Architettura* (1537-51). Serlio (1475-1554) was a pupil of Peruzzi in Rome. Later he travelled to Venice and, after 1540, to France where he worked under the protection of François I. His book was the first lucid attempt to provide a 'parallel' or comparative analysis of the architectural Orders, showing the five different types of column, entablature and capital in one plate. He included plates of work by Bramante, and also used a number of the highly praised drawings of Peruzzi as the basis for others, including the three different types of scenic perspective, as mentioned by Vitruvius. As Vitruvius' text was received without illustrations from the Middle Ages, reconstructions by Serlio, Barbaro, Palladio and Philbert de L'Orme were extremely valuable. Compared to Alberti's treatise of the

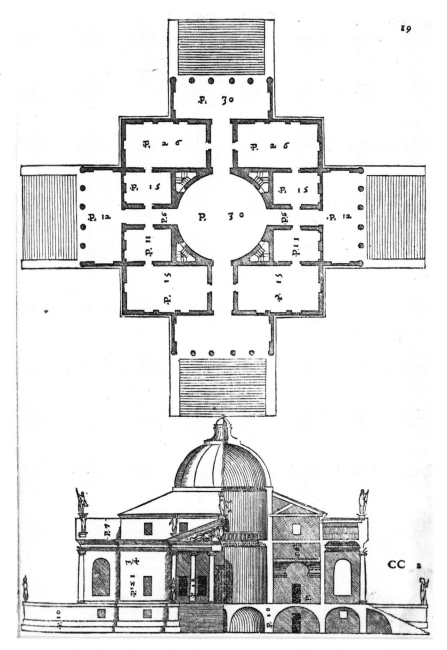

19

CC 2

La Rotunda is the only design built by Palladio that corresponds exactly to its illustration in the *Quattro Libri.* The plan, composed of the simplest and most beautiful geometrical figures, was symmetrical, with each side presenting exactly the same elevation. The central dome expressed the ideal *unità* and *uniformità* of the circle as a visible monumental form, one hitherto confined to sacred architecture. The design was 'ideal'; its perfection was not marred by the usual array of service buildings, and it acted as an abstract examplar that inspired generations of suburban villa builders.

previous century, that of Serlio was a work of popularization rather than scholarship, and immensely successful. In 1611 *L'Architettura* was first translated into English as *The Entire Works of Architecture and Perspective.*

Serlio's treatment of the Orders was superseded by that of Giacomo Barozzi da Vignola (1507-73), whose *Regole della Cinque Ordini* appeared in 1562 with delicate copper-engraved plates. It gave a simple method for drawing the Orders singly or in combination. This work appeared in countless different editions into the twentieth century.

For the *Quattro Libri dell'Architettura* (1570) of Andrea Palladio, woodcuts were used. Palladio did not draw all of the buildings just as they were built: for some he changed dimensions; for others he altered the form. The book was meant to illustrate what he hoped to achieve, not what he was able to achieve. His aims were impeded by factors such as expense, site constrictions, workmanship and time. The numbers and letters which mark rooms and architectural elements indicate the mathematical, proportional and harmonic correspondences between different parts of the whole. Without the book, Palladio's intentions would be difficult to reconstruct or understand. All the illustrations are in the form of plans, elevations and sections, and it is known that Daniele Barbaro, Palladio's patron, disapproved of perspective as 'inaccurate'. Even the half-way measure adopted by Serlio of having a section with half the interior drawn in perspective is avoided. For eighteenth-century editions of the *Quattro Libri* the plates were re-engraved on copper.

Like Palladio's illustrations, the drawings Philbert de l'Orme published in his *Le Premier Tome de l'Architecture* (1567) were woodcuts. But this did not interfere with the popularity of the work. Very different were the thirty-nine freehand 'topographical' sketches which Etienne Dupérac (*c.*1525-1604) engraved on copper and published only a few years later. The techniques of copperplate engraving, which could provide much greater accuracy and refinement than the crude woodcuts, had come to France in the middle of the sixteenth century. Dupérac, architect to Henri IV at Fontainebleau, was

the first native French master. His masterpiece, uncompleted at his death, was a set of copper engravings entitled *I Vestigi dell' Antichità di Roma, Raccolta et Ritralti in Perspettiva* published in Rome in 1575.

The real popularity of copper engravings, however, was due to the topographical publications of Jacques Androuet Du Cerceau (*c.*1516-84), of which the best known is *Les Plus Excellents Bastiments de France* (1576 and 1579). Du Cerceau (who should be distinguished from the rest of his close family which included important architects and engravers) produced aerial views of the great buildings of France. This was an original and important enterprise, constituting probably the earliest attempts at bird's-eye topographical views. Although he drew the buildings in faithful and precise detail, and despite his clear accuracy, Du Cerceau's indication of the site and surroundings, even of the gardens, is usually perfunctory and slight. There is no evocation of atmosphere, or striving after the image of an integral situation as was later to be the case. Contemporary, and in some ways similar, are the cold dissections of Jacques Perret: plans, cut-away and oblique projections of Mannerist designs in his *Des Fortifications et Artifices Architecture et Perspective* (1601). These prefigured the axonometric view, which is the modern draughtsman's system of detachment.

Italian architectural draughtsmanship in the late sixteenth century was led by the spectacular illustrations of Domenico Fontana (1543-1607) in his volume *Della Transportione dell'Obelisco Vaticano,* published in 1589. Fontana was the architect and engineer who moved the obelisk at St Peter's in Rome. His engravings, however, are far more than a demonstration of mechanical ingenuity. They are complex images which marvellously realize the possibilities of the medium.

The Italian Baroque

Gianlorenzo Bernini (1598-1680) and Francesco Borromini (1599-1667), the two figures who dominate the first half of the seventeenth century in Rome, were both exceptional

The *renovatio* of Rome under Pope Sixtus V was intended to be the transformation of the city into the centre of Counter-Reformation Christendom. Under Sixtus the architect Domenico Fontana erected obelisks as focal points at the ends of important streets and in front of great pilgrimage churches. Devout citizens and pious visitors were expected to walk from one obelisk to another, stopping at every shrine, *confessione* and church *en route,* meditating, praying and performing other forms of 'spiritual exercise'.

This drawing by Fontana records one of the most spectacular engineering feats of the late sixteenth century. The obelisk shown here was moved from the north side of St Peter's (where it had existed from ancient times) to the front side, so that it would act as a focal point for that part of the city, and as a sign of the triumph of Christianity over pagan antiquity.

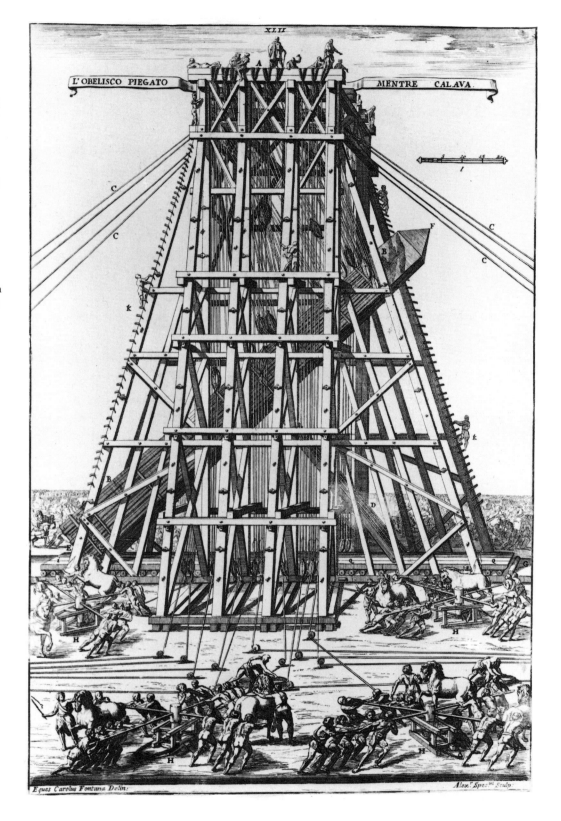

draughtsmen in different ways. Bernini was a fluent and extremely prolific draughtsman who also had an almost miraculous ability to carve in marble. It is as a sculptor that he is best known and it is within this discipline that he received his primary training. However, the main inspiration of his work came from the paintings of artists such as Caravaggio and his followers and Raphael, although he also carefully studied Antique sculpture and its Renaissance interpretations by Michelangelo and others. His sculpture was carved so as to present to the viewer a 'picture' best understood from a single vantage point. In fact, most of his three-dimensional sculptures were made to stand against a wall. This perspectival approach extended to his architecture and his painting. The Cornaro Chapel in the church of Santa Maria della Vittoria is a stunning example of painting, sculpture and architecture combined to create a three-dimensional vision, revealed at a single glance on entering the chapel. The purpose of Bernini's use of perspective was to create the most immediate impact possible. To work out his effects he always made a large number of study drawings which depicted the effects of space and light as a preliminary move to a more precise process of designing. By these means he also delegated work to his numerous assistants. His workshop was the largest and best organized in Rome. His architectural elevations are always inclined to break into perspectives, as in his design for the front of the Louvre (Plate 20). His conception of architecture was tremendously influential and marked the high point of Counter-Reformation Baroque in its exuberance, grandeur and emotionalism. However, by the time of his death the 'illusionism' and 'theatricality' of his architecture was already going out of favour.

Borromini did not practise any arts other than architecture. His background training was in stonemasonry from which he imbibed the traditions of medieval geometry. As a result, he never designed his buildings solely according to Classical 'modules', as was recommended by Vitruvius. Instead he combined this system, and the attendant Classical conception of man and his measurements, with medieval

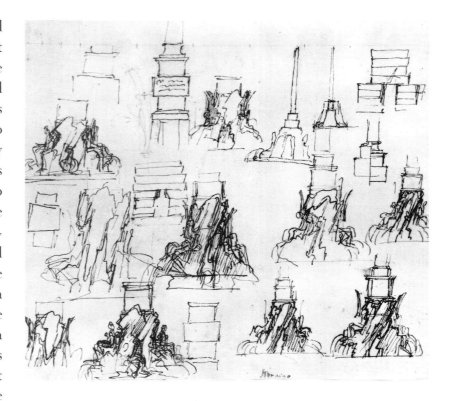

This group of sketches documents Bernini's struggle with the design of the Four Rivers fountain. The art of Bernini, the dominating figure of the Roman Baroque, embodied an idea (*concetto*) that captured the essence of his subject. In this case the *concetto* involved ideas of paradise, the four cardinal directions, the power of the Church and the salvation of mankind. Here we see Bernini interpreting, transforming and coordinating appropriate symbolic forms.

symbolic geometry; for example, with the circle as the image of heaven and so forth. The preparatory drawings for Borromini's first church, S. Carlo alle Quattro Fontane (built 1638-41), demonstrate the ingenious spatiality of his creation, which was controlled by a system of triangulation. By this means all the primary geometrical figures were integrated into the design to achieve a symbolic synthesis. This system was itself integrated into the Classical mode of design. He did not draw perspective sketches but used orthogonal projection. His leanings towards Gothic principles cannot be explained in terms of eclecticism or romanticism. It was a continuity of architectural forms and meanings to which he felt drawn by a deep-rooted affinity. His genius was capable of

This sketch by Borromini, of the façade of S. Carlo alle Quattro Fontane, dates from 1665-7. The division between storeys, the curved façade and rich iconography noticeable in the actual building is not shown here, but wall articulation through the use of columns, pilasters and niches, in relation to different internal spaces, is visible.

adapting these convincingly to the Classical body of forms.

In 1613 the architect Carlo Moderno (1556-1629) sent a letter to Cardinal Barberini (later Pope Urban VIII) which, together with the Cardinal's reply, documents the early seventeenth-century reassessment of perspective as a means of pictorial representation. Moderno had just sent the Cardinal an engraved elevation of the projected West Front of St Peter's, showing Michelangelo's dome rising behind. Like any elevation, Moderno's image was not the same as that which would be visible when the design was built. The elevation represented the geometrical order of the whole composition. However, Barberini complained that Moderno's drawing presented a falsifying effect. The architect explained that a perspective which would show the façade and dome in their perceivable relationship belonged to painters rather than architects because it could not provide exact measurements. The disagreement concerns the problem with perspective illusion. Unlike Bernini, Moderno designed his buildings according to theoretical rather than perceptible criteria. This is not to say that he was uninterested in the appearance of his building. Rather, he had a different approach to the problem of controlling the visible aspect of his building. He believed that geometrical order was superior to empirical order because it represented permanently valid relationships between parts. Empirical order was contingent on an individual's point of view. Moderno believed that this was problematic because multiple viewpoints always differ. The virtue of his elevation was that it transcended rival viewpoints. Although it was imperceptible, it was geometrically correct; in the place of a perspective illusion he provided a drawn concept. The Moderno-Barberini disagreement marks an important stage in the long struggle between these two forms of representation. The struggle was made even more difficult as the century progressed. After Bernini and Borromini came great perspective masters like Pozzo and Bibiena. The contemporary developments in stage and interior design exaggerated the problem. Italian Baroque architects developed the techniques of perspective by using additional vanishing points, multiple objects, corner views and contrasts of light and shade. Yet Moderno's complaint remained: no matter how rich the perspective construction, it was still variable, depending on the point of view.

The later seventeenth century brought about an increasing regularity of drawing style, perhaps under the influence of the engraved elevations which were by then frequently being published. The drawings of Carlo Fontana (1634-1714) in the Royal Library at Windsor show a development from the techniques used in Bernini's workshop, but with an increasing isolation of the drawing on the page. Geometrical guidelines are laid out in black chalk. Brown ink is then applied to show the outlines of the buildings, with grey wash used for shading. A greater range of colour was used than previously, but conventionally rather than representationally, with existing fabric shown in yellow or brown, proposed building in grey, water in blue and brickwork in elevation or plan in red.

A neat and careful drawing style was used from the first in the projects prepared for the competitions of the Accademia di S. Luca from the 1670s. This body, which was the most concerned with architecture of the Italian Academies of Arts, exercised a powerful influence on architectural drawing style and students from all over Europe submitted designs in competition for its medals. The influence of the Accademia di S. Luca spread quickly to France after the establishment of the French Academy at Rome in 1666. It formed the basis of the academic style in France in the eighteenth century and subsequently at the École des Beaux Arts in the nineteenth century. In the Accademia di S. Luca drawings there are a few bird's-eye perspectives in the early years, but these give way to an unchanging pattern of plans, elevations and sections, with shadows accurately cast according to the rules, and a general uniformity of presentation.

French Drawing: Topography and Decoration

In contrast to the architects trained in S. Luca, Pierre Le Muet (1591-1669), a French contemporary, was not an architect but an engraver and publisher. Aiming to bring Du Cerceau up to date, he was not drawing to develop his own creative designs but to educate a public. His images are clear and precise. He produced French versions of Palladio (1626) and of Vignola (1631), while his own *Le Manière de Bien Bastir . . .* of 1623 ran to eight editions. The elevations he draws are simple but cold. A scale is added at the foot and window openings are blacked in.

In the manner of the time the image is abstracted from the Paris street. The virtue of this kind of abstraction is its clarity; the ideas to be communicated can be easily understood.

For generations after Le Muet, the great French draughtsmen appeared in family dynasties, much like the Du Cerceau family already mentioned. Of the Le Pautre family, one became, under Mansard, illustrator to the Royal Buildings, but the family's most memorable contribution to draughtsmanship came from the brothers Antoine (1621-77) and Jean (1617-82). Antoine Le Pautre was one of the most original seventeenth-century French architects and a founder of the French Academy. In his *Oeuvres d'Architecture* (1652) he produced sectional perspectives which give a sense of building materials, construction and detail that surpasses earlier French drawings. Jean Le Pautre, a decorator and engraver, became one of the century's great draughtsmen and undoubtedly its most prolific. Between 1641 and 1680 he published fifty-four works, engraving in his sixty-five years at least two thousand plates. This work has a lightness of touch and vivacity, even if some way from being architectural in the contemporary sense. Nevertheless, Le Pautre saw himself as an architectural draughtsman, but his over-use of every known ornamental device helped feed the reaction against 'Louis Quatorze' style even before the monarch's death in 1715.

Jean Marot (1630-79), a leading architect to that court, is known also as draughtsman for two celebrated publications which are very different from the spirit of Jean Le Pautre. Of these the one best known to history is *Le Petit Marot*. The buildings are expressed with sympathy and conviction, but in the simplest possible way. With elevations, sections and plans, whose modest quality of line is nicely judged for the size of publication (a quality lost if the plates are enlarged), the buildings are turned into little jewels.

Marot's son Daniel (1650-1718?), an illustrator and engraver as well as architect to William III of England, combined his father's precision with Jean Le Pautre's freedom to produce engravings with a mastery of light and shade, with grandeur and vitality.

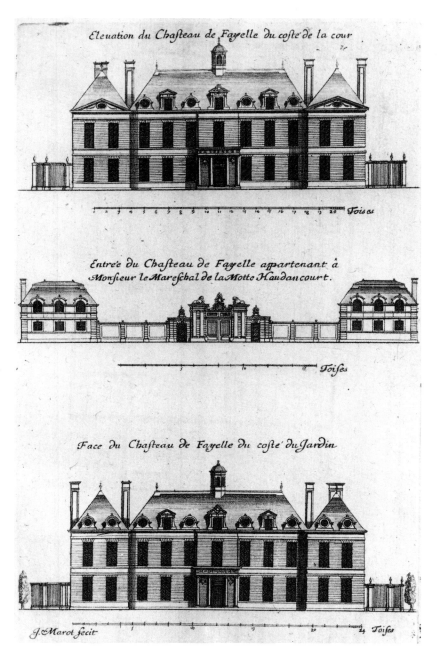

Eleuation du Chasteau de Fayelle du coste de la cour

Entrée du Chasteau de Fayelle appartenant à Monsieur le Mareschal de la Motte Haudancourt.

Face du Chasteau de Fayelle du coste du Jardin

J. Marot fecit

Jacques Bruant, the architect of this chateau, was a competent but undistinguished architect who, like his father, sided with the ancients in the famous *Querelle des Anciens et des Modernes*. The work of both Bruants is always correctly proportioned but rarely innovative. This engraving,

from *Le Petit Marot*, a document that records a wide range of seventeenth-century French buildings, shows the consequences of Bruant's prejudice: architectural conditions, as important as the differences between front and back orientations, are ignored.

The French tradition of architectural topographical draughtsmanship developed as the seventeenth century progressed, and it cannot be passed without mention of the *Grand Cabinet du Roi,* Louis XIV's immense undertaking to record the notable events of his reign. Engaging at one time or another virtually evey contemporary French draughtsman and engraver of note, it actually reached twenty-three volumes of illustrations: plates of towns beseiged, battles fought, and so on. The message may not have been architectural, but it produced some interesting drafting solutions. A typical project may, for instance, have been to represent the capture of a town; the programme demands a plan of the town, a distant perspective view of it, and a verbal description, perhaps supplemented by a portrait of the victorious general. If we look at Charleroy, engraved by Pierre Le Pautre, we see this potentially awkward mixture of images united in a masterly and decorative way. This illustration, in fact, uses four separate plates (which also allowed the border or frame to be used for different illustrations). Besides the Le Pautres and the Marots, one other family, the Perelles (Gabrielle, 1603-77, and his two sons Nicolas, born 1631, and Adam, 1640-95). whose work is barely distinguishable one from another, also worked on the *Cabinet,* producing many of its finest illustrations. Less brilliant was Israel Sylvestre (1621-81) who delineated many of the most important French buildings. The military emphasis shows how the French Army was an important employer of draughtsmen and contributed to the formation of a standardized drawing style.

The new departure, in perspectives of great houses, was to move the sight lines high up, producing bird's-eye perspectives (which Du Cerceau's had never been), showing the *châteaux* in their environment, and suggesting an atmosphere with flair and dexterity. The perspective may be accepted as accurate and the building at one with its context. The foregrounds are managed with skill, and the landscapes and figures are drawn with as much dexterity as the buildings. The whole, in fact, conveys a fine sense not only of place but of the atmosphere of the age.

Architectural Drawing in England

The earliest English architectural drawings date from the reign of Queen Elizabeth I, a time when the concept of a professional architect was tentatively beginning to emerge. Two important collections should be noted: first, the Smythson drawings, by Robert Smythson (1536-1614), his son John Smythson and grandson Huntingdon Smythson; and second, the notebook of John Thorpe (c. 1563-1655) which contains mainly survey drawings of existing houses, which, at one time, were thought to be Thorpe's actual designs. The documentary value of both these collections is enormous, but as drawings they are very elementary, taking the form of plans or 'platts' and elevations or 'uprights' with occasional crude indications of perspective. Nor did the first illustrated English book on architecture, John Shute's *The First and Chief Groundes of Architecture* (1563), rival the Continental publications, although it contained good copper engraved plates of the Orders. The text provided a brief introduction to the history, theory and use of the Orders and a definition of the 'perfect Architecte or Maistre of buildings'. Shute relied heavily on Serlio, whose book was already known in England, for his interpretation of the Orders, but he was also influenced by the perspective manuals of J Vredeman de Vries (b.1527) and the more ornamentally biased works of Wendal Dietterlin (1550-99).

With Inigo Jones (1573-1652) the Classical form of architecture, the Italian mode of drawing and design, and the Renaissance conception of the architect finally took hold in England. The early draughtsmanship of Inigo Jones had been within the formal Elizabethan tradition but within eight years, between 1605 and 1613, he taught himself to draw and become an accomplished exponent of the free line and wash drawing. He was the first British artist to realize the importance of this technique. His style was derived from the paintings of Isaac Oliver (d.1617) and, more immediately, from the engravings of the Italian Mannerist painters, the engraved instruction sheets of the Carracci school and the engravings after Parmigianino, Schiavone, Agostino Carracci and Bacci Bandinelli. Even in

the sketchbook which he took with him on his tour of Italy in 1613-14, known as the *Roman Sketchbook,* the sketches are nearly all from engraved sources. All these artists gave him a vocabulary for his fluid style: dramatic chiaroscuro, elongation of the figure and a sinuosity of line. John Webb records Van Dyck's assessment of Jones as a draughtsman as someone 'not to be equalled by whatsoever great masters in his time for boldness, softness, sweetness, and sureness of touch'.

The most beautiful drawings by Jones include his designs for the masque productions of the Stuart court. The Mannerist engravings and the designs of Giulio Parigi and Jacques Callot were a quarry for his elaborate stage sets and designs for these spectacles. The designs were generally made using the same draughting technique: sketches in lead with a brown wash redrawn in pen and brown ink. The masques were closely modelled on the theatrical spectacles produced for the Medici Grand Dukes of Florence in the 1580s. The stage sets of Jones, following these Renaissance examples, were radically different from the Elizabethan stage conventions of the 'theatre in the round'. He introduced the proscenium arch and the perspectival backdrop which, of necessity, posited an ideal viewing point. Many of the courtiers had to be instructed on how to 'read' the perspective conventions used in the scenery. They presumed, for instance, that the distant figures shown on the horizon line were badly represented flying angels. To learn the 'art of seeing' in perspective they had to sit in the King's chair which was placed to accommodate the ideal viewing position. From this vantage point the logic of the perspective could be explained to them. This conception of space has to be taken into account when one examines the architecture of Jones.

The main sources of Inigo Jones's architectural ideas were the buildings, publications and original drawings of Palladio and Scamozzi. With his acquisition of the *corpus Palladianana* he had first-hand information on how one of the greatest of modern Renaissance architects designed. He learnt the discipline of orthogonal drawing in plan, section and elevation, all of which he executed with a fine pen and delicate

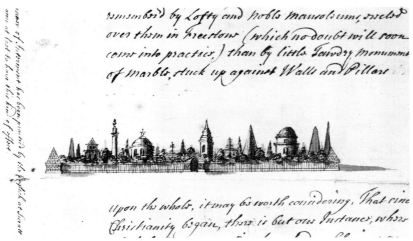

This preliminary sketch by John Webb for a quarter of the Cabinet Room ceiling at Wilton House (top) is clearly intended for an illusionistic or *trompe l'oeil* ceiling decoration, with the depth of space apparently increased by the painted colonnaded gallery. Although now firmly attributed to Webb, this is one of his many drawings which have been wrongly assumed to be by his teacher Inigo Jones.

Vanbrugh believed that the city church should be isolated as a visible monument, while the cemetery should be located at the city's edge. His drawing of an ideal cemetery (above), a mirror image of an ideal city, consisted of pyramids, obelisks and mausoleums interspersed with walks and avenues. The architectural forms came from a spectrum of traditions that combined a density of symbols and aesthetic variety.

washes or with a lively pen, sepia ink and cross-hatched shadows. This discipline, combined with his experience of contriving perspectival stage sets and the painterly effects of the masque, gave the architectural designs and buildings of Jones a Classical conviction which later inspired generations of English architects. His pupil, John Webb (1611-72), was a less fluent draughtsman and architect than Jones. He drew many of Jones' designs but in a neater and more meticulous manner.

Sir Christopher Wren (1632-1723) was the next great English architect after Jones but his method of designing buildings followed a different course. He was a Fellow of the Royal Society and was very interested in the more scientific aspects of architecture such as structural problems, the art of stone cutting and methods of construction. This interest allowed him to develop ties with native craftsmen and their methods of building which flowered in his magnificent combination of the Gothic and the Classical in his churches. Like the next generation of English Baroque architects he did not develop any virtuoso drawing techniques. His elevations for buildings could depict a solidity of modelling and shadow absent from the Palladian drawings (which were more concerned with the representation of proportion and harmonic measurements) but in general his drawings do not convey an image of the three-dimensional plasticity of his buildings. He placed great emphasis on the model as a design aid, in practice if not in theory; the model for St Paul's was one of the finest ever produced. His Baroque successors in England, Sir John Vanbrugh (1664-1726), Nicholas Hawksmoor (1661-1736), Thomas Archer (c.1668-1743) and James Gibbs (1683-1774), did not leave any drawings which fully convey the spatial qualities of their buildings. They followed the Classical convention of orthogonal representation. Hawksmoor occasionally produced perspective sketches of his Gothic designs but generally used the plan, elevation and section. Some rough designs which can be identified as being from Vanbrugh's hand are unusual in their directness and simplicity. Perhaps his most characteristic drawing is his project for an ideal cemetery, full of 'pyramids, arches and obelisks'.

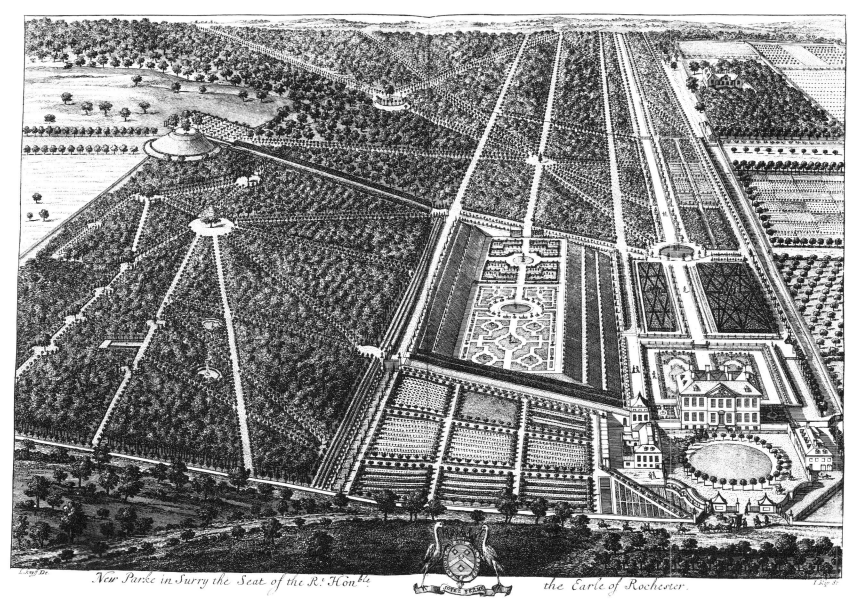

New Parke in Surry the Seat of the R.t Hon.ble   the Earle of Rochester.

Topographical drawing in Britain was usually the province of Continental artists, notably Wenceslaus Hollar (1607-77), whose views of London before and after the Great Fire are well known. Later in the century, David Logan (1633-92) of Gdansk popularized the bird's-eye perspective with his beautiful and often reproduced plates of the university colleges, *Oxonia Illustrata* (1675) and *Cantabrigia Illustrata* (1688). His illustrations were confined to the immediate subject and did not include the surroundings. Twenty years later, the

This engraving was published by Jan Kip and Leonard Knyff in their three-volume *Nouveau Théâtre de la Grande Bretagne* of about 1700. Both Knyff, a draughtsman, and Kip, his engraver, were trained in Holland before they emigrated to London in the 1690s, after the accession of William and Mary. In the late seventeenth century their talents were unsurpassed. Unlike native British artists, Kip and Knyff were

heirs to a well-established tradition of topographical drawing, and their bird's-eye views, such as this one of New Park in Surrey for the Earl of Rochester, were among the first in England to locate their subjects in the surrounding landscape. Though drawn with meticulous care and acuracy, their work was rather stiff and artistically unadventurous, but is nevertheless of great archaeological value.

Dutch engraver Jan Kip (1652-1722) began publication of *Britannia Illustrata* (with a second volume in 1717) from drawings by Leonard Knyff. In their illustrations the bird's-eye views include the landscape surrounding the subject.

Before the turn of the seventeenth century, John Slezer (?-1717), a Dutchman who settled in Scotland, published topographical drawings of Scotland in the folio *Theatrum Scotiae*. The drawings in this folio were executed in a manner similar to those of Du Cerceau. They have, however, an austere, almost naïve quality, which differentiates them from the more studied French examples.

Rococo and Palladian Drawing

When considering the development of architecture in England and France in the eighteenth century, it is all too easy to become entangled in a number of stylistic labels which describe overlapping periods and which have different meanings in each country. As far as the history of drawing is concerned there were certain developments in technique which transcend stylistic categories. One of the most important developments was that of the cartouche sketch. The appearance of these drawings coincided with the origin of Rococo decoration. Unlike pre-eighteenth-century images, they made no attempt to follow the canons of architectural proportion and mathematical rule. Each cartouche was unique. But the uniqueness of the image was not a result of the differences between the objects represented: leaves, animals, natural forms, etc. Rather, it was a consequence of a new interpretation of architectural design; in Rococo design the temporal or developmental character of artistic activity was stressed. Each figure represented a unique moment in the continuous process of artistic activity. This practice differed radically from Classical method which endeavoured to imitate eternal forms such as circles and squares. Where Classical architectural forms were unchanging, Rococo cartouches were always developing. The aim of this kind of design and drawing was to emulate the evolving process of Nature.

The idea of the cartouche sketch was opposed by that of the conventional Neo-Classical representation of a building with the combination of plan, section and elevation. This type of representation, now very common, was formally instituted at this time as a preferred means of drawing. In both France and England Neo-Classical architects opposed what they considered the excesses of Rococo images with cool, crisp and highly objective drawings. This style was popularized by Blondel, Boffrand and their pupils in France, and by Lord Burlington and his followers in England. In France the rejection of Bernini's design for the new front of the Louvre in 1662 marked a change in attitude and a desire for an architecture governed by strong academic rules. Yet, while the external surface or architectural framework of buildings remained strict, the use of arabesque ornament was already beginning to flower into what has been called the Rococo. Thus, Neo-Classicism and Rococo developed side by side, often within the same building. As an ornamental style based on linear decoration, Rococo images lent themselves to reproduction through engraving, and many pattern books resulted. Certain drawings, however, by Vassé, Oppenord and others, showing sections of interiors, are shaded to give a poetic feeling of space and light. Among drawings for exteriors, the brilliant project for the façade of S. Sulpice in Paris by Juste Aurelle Meissonnier (1695-1750) must be mentioned, although the selection of Jean-Nicholas Servandoni's (1695-1766) design for this church was one of the starting points of the reaction against the Rococo in France.

François de Cuvillies (1731-77), a pupil of Jacques François Blondel (1705-74), published designs of his architect father's which are notable for their bold contrasts of light and shadow, and for their expression of texture. He also included much coarse *rocaille* ornament and wild landscape.

Germain Boffrand (1667-1754) published an important collection of designs in his *Livre d'Architecture,* which used, by contrast, a sober technique. In the same period Antoine Babuty-Desgodets (1653-1728) was compiling the carefully measured drawings of ancient monuments in Rome which

Fig. 174.

L'Étable à Vache tournée au midi, est sur la fraîche prairie.

The gradual dissolution of baroque iconology at the end of the eighteenth century had a counterpart in the growing use of liberated images in accordance with individual choice, imagination and differentiated meanings. Jean Jacques Lequeu developed this to the point where the formal vision becomes an almost impenetrable world of private reverie. In his Étable à Vache, shown here, the theme, from the texts of Indian religion, is transformed into a vision of a zoomorphic temple. Typical elements in Lequeu are the cryptic details, in this case the sacrificial vessel on the bull's head and the hidden space under the podium which receives light from the bull's eyes. Together with the text, the mechanically precise drawing anticipates surrealism.

Louis XIV's minister Colbert had commissioned him to undertake. These drawings were later to add weight to the reaction against the 'licentiousness' of the Rococo style in France and the desire to return to the true forms of Classical architecture.

Some guide to the drawing techniques of this time in France is given in Buchotte's *Règles du Dessin et du Lavis* (1722) which shows the influence which military draughtsmanship and surveying were having on civil architecture.

In England the early eighteenth century is dominated by the Palladian movement. This was largely concerned with a desire to remove the influence of Baroque architecture from England by a return to simplified Palladian sources, which

from their adaptation by Inigo Jones in the previous century had acquired something of a quality of nationalism. More nationalist than strictly Palladian was the publishing venture begun by Colen Campbell (d. 1729) called *Vitruvius Britannicus* (1713, 1717, 1725) as this collection of engravings, mainly of country houses and projects for them, contained works by Vanbrugh as well as by Campbell and other orthodox Palladian architects. *Vitruvius Britannicus* is an important source book for the history of the English house and was carried on in further volumes to the end of the century. In it the engravings by Hendrik Hulsbergh and John Rocque were of especially high quality.

One of the most notable draughtsmen of the Palladian movement was William Kent (1685-1748). He began his career as a painter and stuccoist, and then was more profitably diverted into architecture by his patron, Richard Boyle, third Earl of Burlington (1694-1753). Kent anticipated by several decades the Picturesque movement, not only in his free and natural style of landscape gardening, but in his interest (expressed in drawings) in the appearance of buildings in the landscape. He was also a remarkable and fertile designer of decoration in a manner which mixes elements from many different styles, one of his most delightful inventions being the State Barge of Frederick, Prince of Wales (1735), preserved in the National Maritime Museum, Greenwich. Kent's drawings of Chiswick, Holkham, Rousham and other houses and their grounds show not only the effect of trees and cut hedges, garden buildings and statues, but also include people walking about. They are simply executed in monochrome ink and wash, but are full of atmosphere, and show an entirely different concept of the expressive power of architecture from the contemporary bird's-eye views of Kip and Knyff.

To show the effect of decoration in a room, Kent used the technique of a plan, with elevations projected outwards in four directions, like a cut-out model. As architects began to be more concerned with the internal arrangements of houses, and the desire to control the details of panelling, chimney-pieces and other important constituents of rooms, this tech-

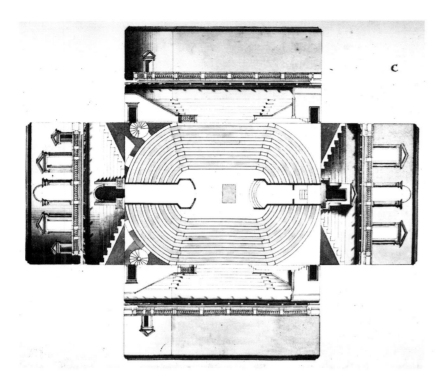

This is one of a beautiful set of proposals by William Kent for the chambers in the House of Commons, London, in which the internal elevations are folded back to the same plane as the floor plan. The drawing is typical of Kent's Palladian style.

nique was increasingly adopted. It was particularly favoured by the Adam brothers.

It is interesting to note that while the two-point perspective of *existing* buildings had abounded in the sixteenth century and become the normal representation for existing buildings by the seventeenth century, it was not until Fischer von Erlach and Filippo Juvarra (1678-1736) that it was consistently used for the designer's own proposed buildings.

The Revival of Antiquity

Desgodets' *Les edifices antiques de Rome* (1682) marked the beginning of a renewed interest in the remains of Classical Antiquity. He was concerned with accurate measurements in a scientific spirit. His findings were used by contemporary theoreticians to criticize some of the prejudices which existed in relation to the proportions of the Orders: specifically, that they were unconditionally beautiful because they were analogous to the proportions of the human body (which is the archetype of all beauty); that they were consonant with the harmonies of music; and, finally, that they determined the universally acknowledged beauty of ancient architecture. Desgodets succeeded in showing that there was no measurable or objective consensus on this matter among the architects of Antiquity, and this set off a series of investigations which succeeded in questioning existing conventions by showing the diversity of proportional order in ancient buildings. An alternative example of the half speculative, half archaeological interest in Antiquity was Johann Bernhard Fischer von Erlach's (1656-1723) *Entwurff einer historischen Architektur* (1721) which showed buildings from all over the world, including some which were presented as ancient but were actually the Austrian architect's own invention. Many of the buildings portrayed by Fischer had never been shown in this way before. Without setting it as his task, he succeeded in codifying the visual history of architecture.

In 1730 Lord Burlington published a collection of Palladio's drawings for the restoration of the Roman Baths. This was called *Fabbriche antiche*. Apart from its importance in the contemporary revival of Antiquity, this publication also indicated Lord Burlington's role as a collector of architectural drawings for their own sake. In the late sixteenth and early seventeenth centuries certain English patrons such as Robert Cecil, Lord Salisbury, had collected architectural drawings and drawings of fortifications, but serious collecting of architectural drawings in England is often thought to have begun with Lord Burlington's legendary acquisition of virtually all Palladio's drawings in the early eighteenth century, including the sheets purchased by Inigo Jones in Italy in 1614.

During the eighteenth century English and French architects and patrons visited Rome in increasing numbers. From the 1740s they found there the man who was to revolutionize the European outlook on the ancient world, and who was to be the inspiration of many of the finest buildings of the second half of the century: Giovanni Battista Piranesi (1720-78), the Italian etcher, archaeologist and architect. Venetian by birth, he came to Rome in search of architectural work, but in fact entered the world of the 'vedutisti', the artists who did paintings and engravings of the ancient and modern sights for sale to tourists and for inclusion in guide books. Piranesi went on to construct his vivid and highly individual vision of Rome as he supposed it to have been in ancient times, adding imagination to the discoveries of the archaeologists. In terms of technique he made great steps forward in the art of etching. His output was phenomenal and he produced more than one plate for each week of his life, many of which were large and very detailed. As well as doing topographical subjects in and around Rome, he had by 1743 produced the plates

Piranesi's drawings for his 'Prisons' series were an unrestrained exercise in architectural fantasy. The nightmare emotions aroused by the image of incarceration and torture were transformed into a visual aesthetic experience through pictorial means. The double diagonal perspective, massive repeating elements and dark framing of the foreground evoke a feeling of crushing yet ungraspable immensity.

for his *Prima Parte di Architetture e Prospettive*. This was a collection of imaginary architectural subjects, similar to those represented in Giuseppe Bibiena's *Architetture e Prospettive*. Piranesi's work differed from that of his contemporaries in its emphasis on archaeological reconstruction. The *Seconda Parte* never appeared, but the *Prima Parte* is full of indications of what Piranesi was to do in the forthcoming years, from grandiose ruins with tiny figures among the debris, to a *Carcere Oscura* foreshadowing his famous series of prisons. Visitors to Rome who had been fired by Piranesi's vision often found the actual ruins rather small when compared to his heroic reconstructions. The influences on his work were many, including Bibiena, Panini, Canaletto, Tiepolo, Tesi, Fischer von Erlach and Marco Ricci. In turn he influenced numerous architects and artists in the eighteenth century and afterwards. He befriended a number of French and English architectural students, including Robert Adam and William Chambers. He actively involved himself in the architectural controversies of the time in particular defending the superiority of Roman and Etruscan architecture over the newly discovered Greek in his *Della Magnificenza ed Architettura de'Romani* (1761). He followed up the same theme in the *Osservazioni sopra la lettera de M Marietta* (1764). In these works, and in the even more extraordinary *Parere sull'Architettura* (c.1767), his illustrations demonstrated his conviction that architecture belonged to both the emotions and the intellect, and this placed him in the forefront of the Romantic movement.

The highpoint of his romanticism, and the work which influenced Coleridge and de Quincy, is the series of *Carceri d'Invenzione* which appeared between 1745 and the early 1760s. The various revisions to the plates made them even darker and more sinister. Architects like Claude-Nicolas Ledoux (1736-1806) and George Dance (1741-1825), who designed prisons in the late eighteenth century, were influenced by this extraordinary vision of Piranesi. In bringing imaginative force to architecture through the use of scale, light and shade, and integration of landscape with architecture, he influenced a wide range of architects.

Adam, Clérisseau, Chambers and Others

As early seventeenth-century Rome was dominated by Bernini and Borromini, so the second half of the eighteenth century in England was dominated by the mutually antagonistic personalities of Robert Adam (1728-92) and Sir William Chambers (1723-96). Both had spent time in Rome and were friendly with Piranesi, who influenced them in different ways. Adam developed from Piranesi his free style of combining different forms and ornament to create unorthodox interpretations of Classical architecture, especially in his original interior work, whilst Chambers restricted his fascination with Piranesi to the enrichment of his drawing techniques and to his garden and mausoleum designs. His project for a mausoleum for Frederick, Prince of Wales, showed the building as a ruin. It revealed a preoccupation with the image of the building in time and as modified by 'nature'; it was a transformation of the Classical conception of architecture and the idea of designing according to the 'immutable' laws of proportion and so forth. It was a portent of the Picturesque theories of architecture. The drawing represented an image of the building in an idealized 'moment' in time. One of the most beautiful drawings by Chambers was a highly rendered cross-section of York House which showed in colour the decoration of the rooms. The elaborate technique of representation owes something to Piranesi but the orthogonal projection and the architecture depicted was equally informed by French influences, with which Chambers was very conversant. He had studied in Paris under Jacques-François Blondel (1705-74) and had learnt the regular and methodical French manner which is evident in many of his drawings and buildings. Chambers was the leading professional architect of his day and was also one of the founders and members of the Royal Academy, from which position he exerted an enormous influence on architectural presentation styles. He also wrote *A Treatise on the Decorative Part of Civil Architecture* which was published in 1759. It ran into many subsequent editions as it became the standard textbook on architecture in England.

In his work Robert Adam fully satisfied the taste for the picturesque while observing the conventions of Neo-Palladianism. He was profoundly inspired by Piranesi's reconstructions of the ruinous grandeur of ancient Rome, learning from him a drawing method which recorded actual and imaginary views and sharpened his aesthetic appreciation of the variety of picturesque composition.

Robert Adam spent longer in Rome than Chambers (supported by his ambitious Scottish family), and although he was an able draughtsman, he also employed the talented Jean Louis Clérisseau. Together they explored the late Roman palace of Diocletian at Split in Dalmatia and in 1764 Adam published a folio volume illustrating his findings. The palace was not a major source of new architectural ideas, but by this time the fashion for archaeological records published by architects had become established, and Dalmatia was considerably easier of access than Greece or Asia Minor.

A large number of drawings from Adam's office survive, most of which are highly finished in colour and show a novel concern with the fittings and complete effect of a room. Indeed, from the 1760s onwards architects paid considerably greater attention to the design of furniture for their interiors and many delightful drawings exist for chairs, sofas, tables and looking glasses.

The engravings in *The Works in Architecture of Robert and James Adam* (1773) are more elaborate than any previous architect's publications of his own work, and include one plate etched by Piranesi as a compliment to his friend (a compliment repeated for another Scottish architect, Robert Mylne, in a splendid plate showing the construction of Blackfriars Bridge). In his written account in this book, Adam stresses the *visual* effect which he desired to achieve – something which would be startling, entrancing, and stimulating to the eye, by a judicious mixture of novelty and precedent. The word 'picturesque' is already used, and he enthusiastically appealed for an architecture which would satisfy the senses as well as the intellect. It was an appeal to add 'variety' to the regular conventions of Neo-Palladianism, making it a lighter, more elegant and unostentatious style.

The lessons of Adam and Chambers were absorbed by a succeeding generation of English architects, including George Dance Jr (1741-1825), James Wyatt (1746-1813) and Henry Holland (1745-1806). However, by this time the differences between the architect's own drawings and those prepared by the office clerks were often hardly noticeable. The clerks were steadily increasing in number and playing an ever more important role in the production of designs and drawings. For example, in Wyatt's office there were a number of draughtsmen to put designs into their finished form, some of whom were members of the large Wyatt family. Henry Holland sent his draughtsman Chatham to Rome to study new 'finds', and recorded (perhaps again with the help of another hand) a number of details and ornaments in exquisite pencil outline in small notebooks for use on projects like the Prince Regent's luxurious rebuilding of Carlton House. Among the drawings done for Dance were magnificent bird's-eye views of his scheme for a new bridge and open spaces east of the Tower of London.

Since standards of architectural drawing had risen so much in the years after 1750, a number of artists emerged who specialized in this work without being practising architects. They combined topographical publishing work with commissions from architects for drawings of projects and frequently set up as teachers as well. Among these were Paul Sandby (1730-1809), his brother Thomas Sandby (1721-98), the first Professor of Architecture at the Royal Academy, and Thomas Malton (1748-1804) who issued a book on perspective, while his son James Malton (*c.*1766-1803) was the recorder of Dublin at the height of its elegance in 1797 in one of the finest sets of aquatints ever published.

Piranesi and the French

The presence of French students in Rome, either as *pensionnaires* at the French Academy, which meant that they had been selected as the most promising young architects of their generation, or merely among those who were making their own Grand Tour, led to Piranesi's ideas being picked up by architects in search of novelty who had the training and talents to put them to good effect. In this way one can trace back to back to Piranesi many of the visual influences which began to change the course of French architecture from 1749 onwards. There was a new concern, both intellectual and visual, for the clear detachment and articulation of parts of architecture. More generally, Italian painting greatly influenced French presentation drawings. In both French and Italian art, columns stood free rather than half buried in the wall as they had been in the Baroque period. At the same time there was an interest in light and shade, in dramatic effects of scale, and in historical narrative, all of which can be related directly to Piranesi's influence.

In these transformations the construction of the church of Ste Geneviève in Paris (now the Panthéon) was crucial. It was designed by J G Soufflot (1713-80), who himself was not a notable draughtsman. However, the building inspired a number of fine engravings by François Philippe Charpentier (1734-1817) and others, as well as a recently discovered wooden model. Jean Laurent Le Geay built less than he drew, and though few examples of his work survive to prove it, he seems to have influenced many of his contemporaries in designing projects on a grander scale. Among these may be mentioned L-J Le Lorrain (1715-60), Charles Michel Ange Challes (1718-78), architect and draughtsman to Louis XV, and N H Jardin. All were students in Rome and found an outlet for their talents in designing temporary constructions for the annual festival called the Chinea. One of the first among this group to emerge as an important architect in his own right was Marie Joseph Peyre (1730-85). His *Oeuvres d'Architecture* (1765) is a collection of grandiose schemes. They are shown in perspective as well as elevation, although not yet with a landscape background. They are mostly exercises in virtuoso planning and composition and, although not built, they were to be influential in the design of public buildings for many years. For his one major building, the Odéon theatre in Paris, Peyre collaborated with Charles de Wailly (1730-98) who deserves to rank as one of the finest architectural draughtsmen of all time. He was as interested in painting and decoration as in architecture. Some of his designs have a distinctly bizarre eclecticism. Peyre and de Wailly produced a building with a stern exterior and a beautiful interior which is perfectly portrayed in de Wailly's celebrated section (Plate 43), showing not only the structure and decoration, but figures moving about in the audience and backstage and out in the street. This drawing marks a new point in the ability to suggest the actual experience of moving through a sequence of spaces in a building. De Wailly's drawing of his extraordinary flying pulpit in the church of S. Sulpice is another *tour de force,* showing his feeling for the drama of buildings in use.

Another great theatre of the 1770s is the Grand Theatre, Bordeaux, by Victor Louis (1731-1800). Many fine drawings for this building survive, and a magnificent folio volume of engravings was also published. The latter stands beside the engravings of Jacques Gondoin (1737-1818) published in the *Description des Écoles de Chirurgie* (1780) as a complete and satisfying record of a new building. It was by means of publications such as these that the French style of public buildings came to dominate Europe in the early nineteenth century.

Among the many fine draughtsmen in France at this time was François-Joseph Bélanger (1744-1818), the stylish architect of the Pavillon de la Bagatelle in the Bois de Boulogne, built for the Comte d'Artois, and Pierre-Adrien Paris (1745-1819), many of whose theatrical and visionary designs are preserved at Besançon.

The Picturesque and the Sublime

The influence of Piranesi's vision in England and France was part of a wider change in ideas about art and attitudes to nature. In England the interest in landscape gardening following the experiments of William Kent, and the interest in non-Classical architecture which went with this, resulted in architectural oddities like Horace Walpole's Strawberry Hill and William Chambers' Pagoda at Kew. These were among the constituents of the Picturesque, which was never exactly a theory of architecture, but rather a series of preferences for architecture which was more visual than intellectual. It stood for the enhancement rather than the suppression of nature, for national differences in style, and a feeling of the individuality of places and their historical associations. There was also a sentimental regard for anything which appeared to be simple, primitive, or otherwise unspoilt by civilization.

These preferences had the effect of making architectural drawings less geometrical and abstract and more concerned with colour, light and atmosphere than they had ever been before. We have already noticed some of these attributes appearing in the drawings of Adam and Chambers and we can follow them in the work of Dance and Wyatt. The rise of the Picturesque coincided with the rise of the English school of watercolour painting, so that much more attention began to be paid to landscape backgrounds in perspectives, and now also in elevations, and in actual building to the setting of architecture in its landscape. The leadership of J M W Turner (1775-1851) and Thomas Girtin (1775-1802) led to a new standard in landscape painting, and among Turner's finest early drawings were views of Fonthill and Hafod, both new buildings which expressed the idea of the Picturesque. Among the watercolours produced for a more strictly professional purpose were those in the *'Red Books'* of Humphrey Repton (1752-1818) which, with seductive coloured pictures, showed the effect of a house and its surroundings before and after its transformation at Repton's command. The Picturesque movement also unleashed a flood, lasting well into the nineteenth century, of books of cottage designs and 'rural improvements', often produced by designers who could attract patrons in no other way. This practice had existed from the early part of the eighteenth century; it began with the publications of architects and gardeners like James Gibbs, Batty Langley and Robert Morris. This development reflects the broadening of the profession and the range of standard building types. In effect, builders who named themselves architects began to consider suburban constructions as architectural objects. For these the newly developed technique of aquatint was perfect for showing textures of plaster and thatch, and for making the humblest building seem exciting by dramatic skies and lighting. Drawings of this sort, beautifully tinted, were published regularly in *Ackermann's Repository,* an all-purpose magazine of the arts, and they were enthusiastically received in other parts of Europe and in the United States.

The Sublime, as opposed to the Picturesque, was first proposed as an aesthetic category in the visual arts by Edmund Burke in *A Philosophical Enquiry into the Origin of our Ideas of the Sublime and Beautiful* published in 1756. It signified the extreme emotions of fear and exaltation felt in the face of things which surpassed normal human dimensions, something which architecture hardly ever does, but which drawings of architecture can suggest. At an extreme level of emotional excitement (and we can best see from the drawings what really set a late eighteenth-century heart beating faster) the Picturesque interest in dramatic effect slipped into the excess of the Sublime, in which 'horrid' was a term of acclamation. Piranesi's work, not only in the *Carceri,* provides a complete vocabulary of Sublime effects, but we may find various aspects of the Sublime expressed in the work of Étienne-Louis Boullée

The elevation and section shown here are designs for Newton's cenotaph by Boullée, who wrote that Newton's infinite genius was best symbolized by a building of this immense scale and perfect form.

(1728-99) and Claude-Nicolas Ledoux (1736-1806). In different ways they carried the influence of Piranesi beyond the scope of their urbane contemporaries whom we have already discussed. Boullée had a small but interesting practice as an architect before the French Revolution, but with time on his hands when politics brought building to a standstill he composed a theoretical *Essai sur l'Art* and drew a number of imaginary schemes to go with it. Boullée's contention was that architecture should be considered as an art with expressive possibilities similar to those found in painting. He used 'painterly techniques' of composition and 'effects' of scale, light and shade to illustrate his architectural ideas. His drawings are surprisingly small in size, considering the grandeur of the subjects he represented. He may have been influenced by the architect and scenic artist Louis Jean Desprez (1740-1804), who made a speciality of the depiction of effects of light, and whose actual scenery survives in the private theatre at Drottningholm Castle, near Stockholm.

Boullée's use of simplified geometric forms – the sphere, cube, cylinder, cone and pyramid – was also characteristic of the later work of Ledoux, notably his customs posts around Paris, the *Barrières,* and the salt works at Arc et Senans in the Vosges. Although he had become *architecte du roi* in 1773 and had worked for Madame du Barry, Ledoux managed to escape the guillotine during the Terror and prepared a massive publication of his work under the title *L'Architecture Considerée sur le Rapport de l'Art, des Moeurs et de la Législation* (1804). An abstruse, theoretical text was accompanied by engravings of his work in which he remodelled his early designs and developed his salt works into a project for an 'Ideal City'. One of the most striking plates in the book illustrated the interior of the theatre at Besançon projected in the eyeball of a gigantic eye. In the others geometrical mass and solidity were emphasized, but it must not be forgotten that in his early career Ledoux designed ornament which surpasses Robert Adam's in delicacy, and in his actual building he never lost a sense of the subtlety of mouldings and projections.

In England the ideas of the Picturesque and the Sublime may be found in the architectural projects of the late eighteenth century. The work of Sir John Soane (1753-1837) in particular may be singled out, partly because his draughtsman, J M Gandy, had extraordinary ability to portray these qualities. Gandy recorded the construction, completion and sometimes even the potential ruination (in Piranesian style) of Soane's work at the Bank of England and elsewhere. One dramatic drawing illustrated an interior in Soane's extraordinary house in Lincoln's Inn Fields, now the Soane Museum.

Among Gandy's other drawings may be noted his *Tomb of Merlin* with its interest in dramatized Romanesque architecture and effects of light. His drawing of *Architecture, its Natural Model,* was equally spectacular. It illustrated the origin of architectural forms in geological and botanical phenomena, a subject that was to interest the Victorians.

Soane's contemporary, John Nash (1752-1835) was not a notable draughtsman, but he employed other capable hands, including George Stanley Repton (1786-1858), son of the landscape gardener, who did the seductive and romantic drawing of the thatched dairy at Blaise Castle, Bristol.

Neo-Classical Germany and the Outline Style

The developments in England and France at the end of the eighteenth century were picked up in Germany, notably by the short-lived genius, Friedrich Gilly (1771-1800), an outstanding draughtsman and designer, whose project for a monument to Frederick the Great (1797) resembles those of Boullée and Ledoux. Some of Gilly's sketches and notes show an astonishing 'modernity' in their use of pure geometrical forms. A fellow pupil with Gilly's father was Karl Friedrich Schinkel (1781-1841), who was pre-eminent in early nineteenth-century Germany as a draughtsman and architect. While Germany was still ravaged by war, Schinkel used his talents as a scene painter, creating a magnificent set of designs for *The Magic Flute* (which he also directed in 1815), and drawing architectural fantasy views, like the one in the *Neue Pinakotek* at Munich, which combine the styles of Piranesi and Caspar David Friedrich. With the revival of Prussia after the defeat of Napoleon, Schinkel started a flourishing practice under Royal patronage. In the projects for buildings which he prepared his careful outlines were matched with atmospheric washes, often in colour. The late drawings for the Palace of the Dowager Empress of Russia in the Crimea, and those for the projected Royal Palace on the Acropolis, present the architecture in a picturesque setting which does not diminish its force. For publication, Schinkel used an austere outline style

This drawing of the Altes Museum, Berlin, by its architect, Schinkel, is a fine example of the outline style of engraving frequently used in the early nineteenth century. It shows the staircase behind the magnificent double colonnade of the portico, which links the inside of the building with the outside. Schinkel, the greatest German architect of the nineteenth century, was influenced by the style of Gilly.

With Schinkel, the outline style of engraving reached a new level of expressiveness, of which the most notable example is the plate showing the view from inside the portico of the Altes Museum in Berlin in which, as in the drawings of Charles de Wailly, the figures help us to see how the building might be experienced. There is hardly any shadow and a uniform bright light is assumed. The people are carefully placed to make contact through the masterly composition. Moving up the stair, heads turn round to look up to the landing and out of the picture plane, or peer round the edge of the balcony, as if off the edge of a great ship, back through the plane of the image into the open space beyond.

The École des Beaux Arts

The teaching of architects at the École des Beaux Arts in Paris from 1819 to 1968 provides a persistent theme in the history of both architecture and styles of drawing.

The school owed its form and traditions to the accumulated French expertise in Classical architecture from the time of Louis XIV, which had succeeded in shifting the centre of architectural innovation from Italy to France, where for many it remained until well into the twentieth century. Until the Revolution, the *Academie Royale d'Architecture*, housed in the Louvre, provided the basis for the study of architecture in France, but in association with it, architects opened private teaching studios (*ateliers*) in which drawings could be prepared under supervision. One of the most famous of these was the school of J F Blondel, whose *Cours d'Architecture* (1771-77) provided the essentials of what an architect of the time was expected to know.

In the following decade, a teaching studio was maintained by E-L Boullée, one of whose pupils was J-N-L Durand. In the closing years of the *ancien régime* the head of the Academy School was David le Roy (who had published the first account of the buildings in Athens), while the Academicians, chosen for their eminence, sat in judgement over the more important competitions, particularly the *Grand Prix de*

of engraving, which was similar to the style used by both Flaxman and Karstens for their illustrations of the Greek classics. The graphic style of these illustrations imitated the drawings on recently discovered Greek vases. In turn it had been used by the French architects Charles Percier (1764-1838) and Pierre-François-Léonard Fontaine (1762-1853), for plates of 'Empire' style ornament, and in England by Thomas Hope in the publication of interiors of his house in Duchess Street, in *Household Furniture* (1807). A similar style was used by J N L Durand as a reductivist approach to teaching architecture and by the draughtsmen Krafft and Ransonnette in their valuable records of Parisian houses entitled *Plans, coupes, élévations de plus belles maisons . . . à Paris* (1802). This style survived until it was replaced by lithography and photographic reproduction, but it has recently been revived under the leadership of James Stirling, perhaps because it is well adapted to the modern stylographic pen.

This detail elevation in grey wash of an Ionic capital for a proposed restoration of the Roman Coliseum was a fourth-year project by Louis Duc, a student at the École des Beaux Arts and a friend of Labrouste. Here the Ionic Order is reduced to a machine-like precision in the sharp mechanical rendering technique of the Beaux Arts. Students were encouraged to study the aesthetic elements separately from the construction of a building. The firmness and simplicity of line and the carefully cast shadows represent the formal aesthetic qualities of this design. The emphasis on Neo-Classical forms at the École had an influence which went far beyond the school itself.

Rome, which provided a four-year visit to Rome and a strong certainty of future work.

This organizational framework was too deeply rooted to be seriously upset by the Revolution, although all the institutions changed their name, and a new approach to architecture was taught at the new École Polytechnique (intended for engineers) by Durand, resulting in his famous reductivist diagrams of different building types. The old Academy School came through to be renamed the École des Beaux Arts in 1819, when it was set up together with the national schools of painting and sculpture.

What, then, were the dominant characteristics of Beaux Arts drawing and how did they arise? The first thing which strikes one about the drawings is that while they were produced as artistic objects in their own right, they acknowledged conventional means of representation: plans, sections and elevations, not perspectives. At any period, the work of one student is hardly distinguishable from that of another, for individuality was valued less than conformity to an accepted set of standards.

Although the drawings reflect changes of taste brought about in the course of the century, they are nearly always Neo-Classical in style, and reflect a consistent doctrine of axial planning, and a particular attention to the artistic quality of the plan as a piece of graphic design. It was the plan which won or lost a competition, and everything else was subsidiary to it. Certain words were used to describe aspects of plans, such as 'poché', meaning the density of solid wall shown on the plan, ranging from the extreme solidity of the prison to the extreme lightness of a Salle des Fêtes. There was also the 'marche', which was considered in relation to the section, and meant the sequence of spaces, or the feeling one would have on walking through the building.

The moral quality attributed to planning in the twentieth century is the direct outcome of the tradition of the École des Beaux Arts, which was imitated in Britain and the United States for teaching architecture. Le Corbusier's phrase 'the plan is the generator' is only a repetition of the traditional

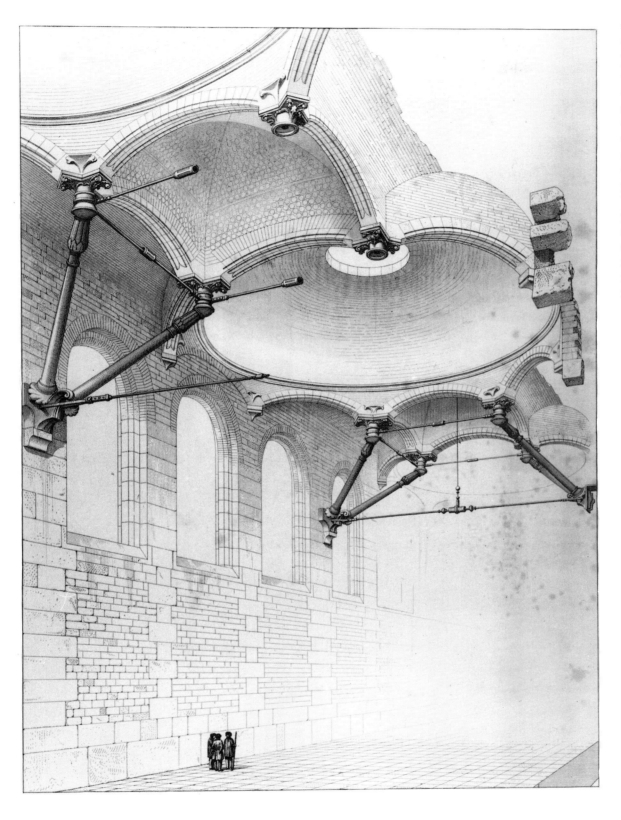

This drawing, like many of those by Viollet-le-Duc, illustrates the split in late-nineteenth architectural thought between stylistic considerations (imitation) and structural considerations (technology). Many contemporary architects were preoccupied with the manipulation of decorative motifs (composition). Opposed to this practice, Viollet suggested 'functional principles' which permitted, even encouraged, the substitution of new materials (especially cast iron) for traditional materials, despite stylistic irregularities and impoverished representational content.

method of the École, although he translated it into different visual terms. Beaux Arts drawings were suited less for the constructions of buildings than for exhibition. All the drawings are done to orthographic projections, but in order to give a greater feeling of depth and texture, all the shadows were carefully cast, even on the plan, and a landscape background was frequently included in the elevations.

To account for these peculiarities of drawing, it is important to remember that these drawings were done as conscious didactic exercises, and the buildings which they portrayed were not necessarily intended to be built. It must also be remembered that although the drawings give little information about construction (all the solid parts of the section being tinted a delicate pink regardless of actual materials), construction was an important subject of study, and was tested in separate competitions.

The competitive nature of the school curriculum, in which the student advanced by gaining a certain number of points in monthly competitions, accounts for the attention paid to draughtsmanship, as it was necessary to catch the jury's eye with a well presented scheme. The visual element always took precedence, as when the aged Charles Percier settled the debate over the award of the *Grand Prix de Rome* in 1824 in favour of Henri Labrouste when, after a quick survey of the plans, he declared, 'Il faut juger aux yeux' (one must judge by eye). By its consistent visual standards, the École des Beaux Arts survived the attacks of Viollet-le-Duc, who saw it as the principal barrier to the reform of architecture. By the vigour of its visual tradition, it also persisted during long periods in the late nineteenth century when there was little progress in the development of architectural thinking. The consistency and assurance of the work done there as much admired by American architects and patrons, particularly after the 1880s when the practice of McKim, Mead and White started to build in a French Neo-Classical manner. A steady stream of American students went to Paris, while many American schools of architecture had French teachers. Later, the English felt that the École might be able to supply what

was lacking in their own educational system, particularly a non-perspective (which meant a non-illusory or honest) form of representation, and until the 1940s many architectural schools in Britain were loosely modelled on the French system.

What was never imitated outside Paris was the system of *ateliers* which was one of the École's great strengths. These continued from the eighteenth century as self-governing 'co-operatives' where the students managed the running of the premises under the patronage of a well-known architect, usually a former winner of the *Prix de Rome*. The École was responsible for formal teaching and examining, but the teaching of drawing went on in the *atelier*. The procedure was that for each 'Concours', a preliminary drawing or 'esquisse' would be done 'en loge' (in a cubicle at the School). The final drawings, which would be delivered two weeks or a month later, had to conform in broad outline to the *esquisse*, in order to show that the student was not cribbing his ideas. Otherwise, the scheme was prepared in the *atelier*, and advice might be given by or sought from other students. Senior students working on large projects would traditionally employ the younger ones to do the hack work on the drawings. The '*Maître*' of the *atelier* would make regular but infrequent tours of inspection, and do his best to make sure that the juries recognized his pupils' work.

For the winner of the *Grand Prix de Rome* the state paid for four years in Italy, based at the Villa Medici, but he was expected to send back 'envois', sets of drawings showing his progress in surveying and measuring the ancient buildings, and drawing out hypothetical restorations of them. Like the prize drawings, these restorations are not only beautiful as artistic objects, but often contain the seeds of important architectural ideas. In this the Americans, and later the English, emulated the French by establishing national schools in Rome.

Victorian England

When Soane and Nash died in the 1830s the Neo-Classical tradition, then in its Greek Revival phase, was still dominant.

This situation was not to last, however, as other styles and doctrines of architecture were beginning to challenge the orthodoxy. In the competition for the design of the new Palace of Westminster, held in 1836, it was recommended to competitors that the 'style' should be Gothic or Elizabethan. Some of the submissions were Neo-Classical, like that of C R Cockerell, but most were in the Gothic idiom. The winning design was by Sir Charles Barry (1795-1860), a fine Neo-Classical architect and draughtsman, aided by the young A W N Pugin (1812-52), whose knowledge of authentic Medieval detail was considerable. The parallel development of the Neo-Classical (Roman and Greek) and the Gothic (which could include Elizabethan or Jacobean) continued through the 1840s, but their co-existence was not unquestioned. Pugin, through books such as his *Contrasts* (1836 and 1841), claimed that only a single style of architecture was possible at any one time, and that the right style for that time was Gothic. He developed a deliberately archaic and unsophisticated style of drawing using rapid sketchy pen lines, which owed much to his study of the works of Dürer and Hollar. He employed it in *Contrasts* to demonstrate the variety and richness of detail in Medieval building as opposed to the austerity and symmetry of Neo-Classical architecture, such as that of William Wilkins and Sir Robert Smirke, which was usually rendered in rather more polished drawings. When the great Gothic architect Sir Gilbert Scott (1811-78) first read Pugin he was so impressed by the moral clarity of Pugin's stance that he said that he felt like someone 'awakened from a long and feverish dream'. By the 1850s the crusading enthusiasm of the adherents to the Gothic doctrine, in opposition to the Neo-Classical, created a situation known as the 'Battle of the Styles'. The debate, however, was not confined to England. Battles also raged in France and Germany.

Among the Neo-Classical designers of the early Victorian period, C R Cockerell stands out as a draughtsman of unusual ability. His mastery of Classical proportion and detail informed even the roughest of his sketches which, however loose, were never clumsy. His finished perspectives were

This interior elevation by Pugin for St George's Roman Catholic Cathedral in Southwark, London, reflects his devout commitment to a High Gothic architecture as the true representation of Catholicism. His deliberately fast and sketchy style emphasizes the elaborate nature of Gothic forms, which he favoured for moral as well as aesthetic reasons.

meticulous in their technique: like other Victorian perspectivists he often depicted the foreground and surroundings of his building and populated the setting with pedestrians, horses and carriages. His drawing of the British Fire Office (1832) design portrays people rushing out of the picture as if towards the scene of a fire. His unsuccessful competition entry for the Royal Exchange (1840) included one of the finest examples of

George Gilbert Scott was a great admirer of Pugin, and his style reflected his Gothic sensibilities. He restored a large number of churches and was also prolific as a secular architect. He designed the hotel at St Pancras Station, London, one of the largest High Gothic structures in the world. This interior perspective is of the hotel's coffee room.

could produce accomplished watercolour perspectives, although he often employed the older convention of the bird's-eye view in a lineal style to illustrate the plan as well as the detail of his larger architectural projects. His main output was of working drawings for buildings, furniture and ornamental work, all of which he drew himself with phenomenal energy. The same attention to working drawings characterized the practice of William Butterfield (1814-1900), whose drawings convey the same precision and practicality evident in his buildings. One of the greatest Gothic Revival architects, GE Street (1824-81), never allowed his assistants to design a single detail in any of his buildings. This attitude was in marked contrast to that of Scott, who was reputedly vague about the authorship of his designs. Nonetheless, Scott was a fine draughtsman.

Scott, Butterfield and Street were successful architects, trying to make Gothic the 'modern' style of the nineteenth century. They were not romantic dreamers like William Burges (1827-81), who seems to have lived spiritually in an Arthurian fantasy world although he carried on an efficient practice. He filled vellum sketchbooks with drawings in the manner of Villard d'Honnecourt, whose original drawings had been reproduced by lithography in 1858, and recommended a 'good strong thick bold line'. Burges was also influenced by Viollet-le-Duc in his style of drawing and design. Following the practice of the École des Beaux Arts, although for very different reasons, he dismissed perspective drawings showing a building as seen from normal eye level, preferring instead the bird's-eye view. Axel Haig produced a particularly marvellous example in his illustration for Burges' competition design for the Law Courts in London. Seen from above, the buildings look like a small city, its towers caught in the sunlight. However, for important competitions, Burges was prepared to commission seductive perspectives.

Alfred Waterhouse (1830-1905), the architect of Manchester Town Hall and the Natural History Museum, London, specialized in buildings of technical complexity for which a large number of efficient working drawings were necessary.

an architectural perspective. The drawing (Plate 49) was accurately and delicately delineated with a convincing rendering of light and shadow. It had a sense of scale and solidity enhanced by the setting of busy city streets. This impressive perspective was lithographed and published along with a view of the interior. Beautiful perspective drawings were also produced by another Neo-Classical architect, Harvey Lonsdale Elmes (1814-47), in conjunction with his scheme for St George's Hall, Liverpool (which Cockerell completed on Elmes' untimely death). One particularly bold and expressive watercolour sketch portrayed the great monumental mass of the building as though lit by the early morning sun and enveloped in a sea-mist.

Pugin was capable of employing several styles of drawing. His design sketches and satirical drawings use what William Burges was to call contemptuously the 'flick and dot' style with loose pen strokes. For presentation drawings he

However, he also produced his own extremely fine perspectives. Having been elected to the Royal Academy on the strength of his architecture, he used to annoy the other Academicians by sending in landscape watercolours to the annual exhibition.

Outside the Gothic movement, mention must be made of Alfred Stevens (1818-75). Although a sculptor rather than an architect, he produced a number of architectural designs in the rich Renaissance and Mannerist style of Cockerell, of

Although his buildings were predominantly Neo-Gothic in style, Alfred Waterhouse did not follow a stylistic or archaeological dogma. To him the value of Gothic architecture was that it allowed flexible planning, as the elevations could be treated asymmetrically and informally. Waterhouse planned his buildings as functional solutions to problems, developing the elevation to suit; that is, he selected style on a functional

basis. He designed as a Quaker, in that he neither believed in a governing body of the church nor the absolute authority of the traditions of architectural representation. He based his designs on convenient planning made legible in the façades, a process well demonstrated in his large and accurately drawn perspectives such as this one of Gonville and Caius College, Cambridge (1867).

which the Wellington monument in St Paul's Cathedral, a brilliant piece of architectural design, is one. Another non-architect was Owen Jones, who was associated with Henry Cole in the attempt to improve design in industry. He composed the elaborate chromolithographed *Grammar of Ornament* (1856), a compilation of decorative motifs of all countries and periods, from which it was hoped that a new synthetic style of ornament would emerge. It was thought by some that this was necessary in order that architects should hold their own against engineers, who seemed to be usurping their traditional function and in the process producing some particularly fine working drawings unencumbered by the stylistic aspirations of professional architects.

Late Nineteenth-Century Drawing

The generation which followed the original Gothic revivalists began in the 1870s to explore different styles, feeling that it was legitimate to make use of anything from history which suited their purposes, and to combine the traditions of different countries and periods in one design. Their work acquired the nickname 'Queen Anne', and soon developed into a very popular style. R Norman Shaw (1834-1912) was one of the leaders of this movement, and was himself a highly accomplished perspectivist in pen and ink, as well as the producer of many sketches. His contemporary Ernest George (1839-1922) noted building details in his tours of the Low Countries, and found ways of reusing them in his Chelsea town houses. He reputedly designed buildings in perspective before working out the plan; something which is an anathema to the Classical method. Shaw's friend W Eden Nesfield was one of the best draughtsmen of his time, having been taught by J D Harding, and his sketches and travel drawings show his keen eye for architectural detail.

One architect who did not share the 'sketcher's' pictorial attitude to architecture was Philip Webb who inherited from the previous generation a belief in the moral seriousness of architecture, and produced nearly all of his own working drawings. Apart from his architectural work, however, he drew beautiful birds and animals which were used by his friend William Morris as decorative motifs. Another 'non-sketcher' was the church architect G F Bodley (1827-1907) who, instead of drawing old churches, would simply look at them for the length of time it took to smoke a cigar, and thus memorize all the details.

An attempt to impose greater discipline on English architectural drawing was made in the teaching at the Royal Academy Architectural School, whose master from 1870 was R Phené Spiers. He was in outlook more of a draughtsman and historian than an architect, and one of the few Englishmen trained at the École des Beaux Arts. Spiers' book *Architectural Drawing* (published in 1887) gives instructions on students' work, office work and outdoor work, recommending the French style of rendering, but seeing advantages also in current English practice.

One of the finest draughtsmen of the 1880s was A Beresford Pite (1858-1937) who sprang to fame by winning the RIBA's annual Soane Medallion with his 'Design for a West End Clubhouse', a beautifully drawn Burgesian fantasy (Plate 68). Pite's drawings of north German towns appeared frequently in *The Builder* in the 1880s, and for his own remarkable buildings he often prepared impressive pen and ink perspectives. The drawings of C F A Voysey (1857-1941) are often attractive for their plainness and for the use of a limited range of colours. As with all architects of the Arts and Crafts movement, his working drawings show an interest in materials and methods of construction as well as being attractive in their own right. Voysey is often bracketed with Charles Rennie Mackintosh (1869-1927) as a pioneer of modern architecture, although their intentions were not the same as those of later architects. Mackintosh's style, like that of his Continental *Art Nouveau* contemporaries, is strongly influenced by oriental art, so that even his perspective drawings have a sort of flatness. His drawings could be described as an architectural equivalent to those of Aubrey Beardsley. Mackintosh's later years were spent doing watercolours of landscapes and flowers, which

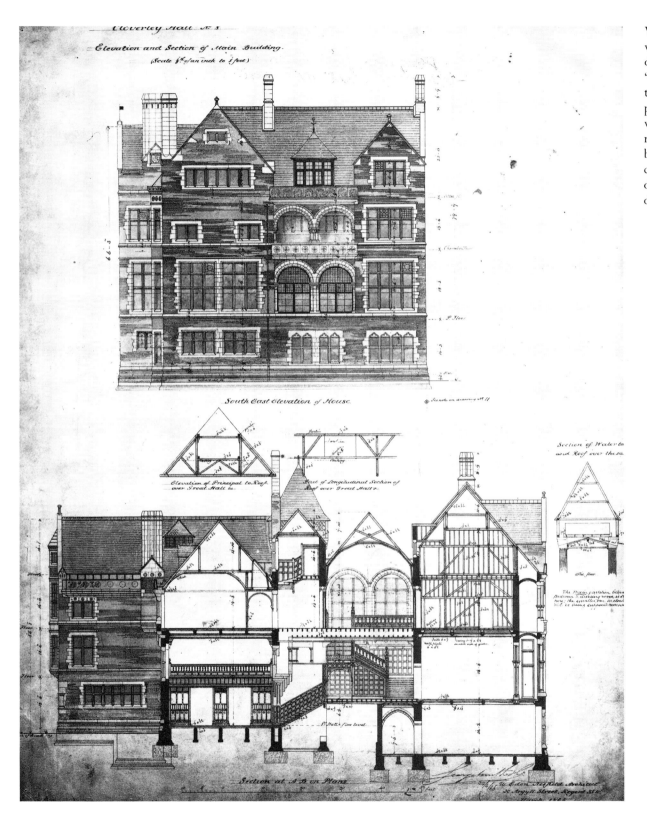

W Eden Nesfield and Norman Shaw were instrumental in the development of the 'Old English' and 'Queen Anne' styles. Their sketching technique, which captured the picturesque qualities of English vernacular architecture – hipped roofs, dormers, chimney stacks, brick detailing and so forth – was carried over into their construction drawings, as can be seen in this early design by Nesfield.

Dated 1905, these referential sketches of a barn at Saxlingham are on a typical page of Mackintosh's sketchbook. Done in pencil, the overlapping images of elevations and perspective have been carefully observed and fastidiously recorded. For another, earlier, example of Mackintosh's drawing style, see Plate 72.

show an architect's sense of form and are most delicately coloured.

In America, the 1870s and 1880s were dominated by Henry Hobson Richardson (1838-86), an architect of tremendous originality and ability who had been trained at the École des Beaux Arts. From the École he adopted the method of doing tiny rough studies to give the impression of a building, which were afterwards worked up by his staff under verbal instruction. His surviving autograph drawings are nearly all of this type. The same method was used by J J Burnet (1857-1938), a Glasgow architect who had also been at the École. One of the draughtsmen on whom Richardson relied heavily was the brilliant, volatile Stanford White (1853-1906) who joined forces with another Richardson assistant and ex-Beaux Arts man, Charles McKim (1847-1909) to form the partnership of McKim, Mead and White. In many ways this partnership became more influential than Richardson himself, since its members introduced French design techniques which formed the dominant American style from the 1890s to the 1920s. One of the few architects to withstand their influence and continue to work in what he felt to be the genuine American style was Louis Sullivan (1856-1924), who must certainly be reckoned among the great draughtsmen, particularly for his sparkling designs for ornament and pattern, drawn with a soft pencil in something approaching the 'dazzle' technique.

Nineteenth-Century Publications

Important changes in architectural draughtsmanship through the nineteenth century were set off by professional and constructional changes, by the development of the drawing as a legal contract document, and by the growing profusion of working drawings. Even more profound was the development of techniques for reproduction of drawings.

Office techniques were revolutionized by the development of tracings and the blueprint duplicating process of the 1870s. However, much earlier in the century the publication of drawings was revolutionized by the arrival of lithography which immensely cheapened the cost compared to the earlier techniques of copper and steel engraving.

In lithography a greasy image on smooth limestone is moistened and inked, the image repelling water and accepting ink, the stone accepting water and repelling ink. This technique came into its own with the work in England of

CJ Hullmandel (1789-1850) and the magnificent railway prints of JC Bourne in the 1830s. (These, like the best copper and steel engravings of the period, were sponsored by the topographical publisher John Britton.) It was quite easy for non-specialists to learn lithography; Norman Shaw drew his *Architectural Sketches from the Continent* directly on stone in 1858.

Chromolithography, a slow and painstaking process for producing coloured prints, developed in the 1830s and 1840s. It is particularly linked with architectural draughtsmanship by its expert use in the work of Owen Jones.

Jones' 1836 chromolithographs of the Alhambra are the best early examples of this art, in which flat colours are printed with tonal effects achieved by stippling or by zigzag lines, by local shading, colour and tone, and by use of transparent and graduated tints. With a set of Hullmandel's published architectural chromolothographs in 1839, the publisher noted: 'This is the first and as yet only attempt to imitate pictorial effects of landscape and architecture in chromolithography', and the technique developed further in the illustrations (by Owen Jones and others) for John Weale's *Quarterly Papers in Architecture* (1844-5). But in the most famous chromolithographic book, *Grammar of Ornament* (1856), Jones returned to a style of flatter colour. The technique, too expensive and awkward to use, developed no further.

Examples of its charming use for architectural reproduction continued, however, and are typically seen in the *Architektonischer Skizzen Buch* which published current German designs in small instalments for around thirty years from 1853. Here, in an early volume, sheets of house designs were arranged with their elevations in soft chromolithographic colours above plans drawn in line only. In a later volume not only is the cool, flat colour effect manipulated to advantage, but the pages are filled with flat decoration, very much in the manner of Jones' *Grammar of Ornament*.

In the large number of architectural journals which began to appear in Britain and Europe from the 1840s onwards, wood-engraving was the medium used for illustrations. Reproductive engraving of line drawings reached a peak of technical achievement in the nineteenth century. Orlando Jewitt was one of the most noteworthy draughtsmen and engravers who contributed work to *The Builder*. Another was HW Brewer who specialized in large imaginary bird's-eye views of medieval cities. Journals in France like César Daly's *Revue Générale d'Architecture* and *La Construction Moderne* were similarly illustrated. In the 1880s in England, wood-engraving began to be replaced by the cheaper but not necessarily more effective 'ink photo' process which could reproduce wash drawings directly, or illustrations specially drawn on lithographic plates, which often lost the quality of the original. At the same time, photolithography allowed the fluent pen-and-ink drawings of Norman Shaw and his followers to be reproduced directly. Their brilliant use of line, anticipating 'dazzle' technique, sometimes prompted the suspicion that they kept specially notched T-squares for drawing irregular lines of roof tiles. Perspectives of proposed buildings were the main contents, but there were also orthographic drawings, mostly plans and elevations. In the later part of the century it was often draughtsmen like Maurice B Adams of the *Building News,* and T Raffles Davison of *The British Architect,* who edited the journals. Adams ran the Building News Designing Club, to which young students and pupils could submit their work for comment and publication, while Davison produced an enormous number of drawings in pen and ink for his own and other magazines.

For books on architecture like Parker's *Glossary,* Gwilt's *Encyclopaedia* and Viollet-le-Duc's *Dictionnaire Raisonnée,* wood-engravings were incorporated in the text, although lithography might be used for full plates. In the early editions of Ruskin's *Seven Lamps of Architecture* (1849), the illustrations were printed lithographically from etchings which Ruskin himself had prepared. They gave a dramatic impression of deep shadows and crumbling textures which could not be obtained in any other medium.

The advent of photography inevitably altered the illustration of existing works of architecture. The Architectural Photographic Association (later Society) was founded as early as 1857, to promote the 'sharpness and precision . . . of the delineation of buildings', through photography. Experiments with photomontage during the design stages were occasionally attempted but this did not really develop until the twentieth century. Meanwhile, another nineteenth-century institution, the architectural design competition, was changing the ethos of the presentation drawing.

The Influence of Architectural Competitions

Architectural competitions were not an innovation of the nineteenth century but they acquired a new role and importance which deeply affected the production of architectural drawings. Previously the normal role of the presentation drawing was to sell the scheme to a particular client. With the competition the judges and, ultimately, the general public who would see the winning schemes on exhibition or reproduced in the magazines, had to be convinced of their worth. Through the offices of the competition and the exhibition, the architects and draughtsmen of the nineteenth century wooed and courted the general public in a hitherto unprecedented way. Their subjects were provided by the new public buildings which were needed in almost all the major cities of the Western world. Competitions were held for the design of town halls, law courts, government offices, workhouses and other public buildings.

In 1835 in Britain ninety-seven designs were submitted in the competition for rebuilding the Palace of Westminster. In 1857, a year during which sixty-nine public competitions were advertised, two hundred and eighteen entries were received in the mismanaged competition for new Government Offices in Westminster. By the end of the century competitions were regularly held for almost all new public buildings, whether large town halls or small public libraries, and they were an effective way for a young outsider to establish an architectural reputation.

Competitions greatly encouraged the perspective drawing. Although the substance of a design had to be conveyed by geometrical drawings – plans, elevations and sections – almost

This 1866 competition entry for the National Gallery, London, by Matthew Digby Wyatt, shows Wyatt's use of convincing and atmospheric perspective to lend an air of authority and visual coherence to his designs, which depended for their appeal on a concrete evocation of architectural 'mood' through the imitation of different kinds of architectural features. Wyatt designed in an assortment of styles, and his eclecticism reflected his abilities as an architectural scholar and his belief that 'style' was secondary to 'structure'.

all competitions allowed the submission of a perspective or 'artist's impression' of the completed building to give both judges and public an idea of its quality. The rebuilding competition for the National Gallery, London, and the competition for the Law Courts, both held in 1866, elicited some of the largest and most accomplished perspectives ever drawn.

By the end of the century, the services of a good perspectivist were essential in competition work, the architect himself usually having neither the time nor skill to make them. This led to the employment of 'ghosts' or 'renderers', a group dealt with at length below. Although these perspectives were usually unsigned, certain draughtsmen were sought after for this work, particularly Stanley Davenport Adshead (1868-1946), for example. In the limited competition for the Old Bailey five out of the six perspectives submitted were found to be by Adshead – to the great surprise of each of the competitors!

This, at least, helped to put all the competitors on an even footing, as it was widely felt that to have stylish and exaggerated perspectives in competitions was unfair, as they distracted attention from the real merits of a design. In the Palace of Westminster competition the condition was made that only three perspectives were allowed. These were to be drawn from specified viewpoints and executed in monotone. Such sensible conditions were rare, however, and the artistic licence of many perspectives added to the general unease with the mismanagement of many competitions. In 1900 the RIBA decided that perspectives were unnecessary in competitions and by the 1920s they had virtually disappeared – except from the walls of the Royal Academy – and only geometrical drawings were submitted in architectural competitions.

The 'Renderers'

Competitions, however, were not the only factor which favoured the use of the 'ghost' perspectivist or 'renderer'. Changing conditions of practice in the nineteenth century led to the architect's role becoming more that of an administrator and businessman than it had been before. This, together with advances in the technique of reproducing drawings, produced a new figure in architectural drawing, the 'renderer' or perspective artist whose task, apart from competition work, might vary from providing an attractive drawing to please the client or publicize the architect, to the actual designing of the elevations of a building. These men were usually freelance, and although they may have had training as architects they did not actually build much, or at least not under their own name. In England the covert designing was known as 'ghosting', while the preparation of perspectives was known as 'taking in washing'. For young draughtsmen on both sides of the Atlantic it provided a source of independent employment even though they had been unable to set up a practice on their own account.

A particular type of draughtsmanship developed in America in the 1880s was known as 'dazzle technique', since it relied on an effect of strong light created by wavy lines. Its American practitioners included Martin Rico and Henry P Kirby (1853-1915), while in England it was developed by C E Mallows (1864-1915) and his pupil Robert Atkinson (1883-1952). Its equivalent in terms of watercolour was the style of William Walcot (1874-1943), whose 'dissolving visions of Portland stone' were popular with Edwardian architects, and whose style was much imitated. Walcot was also a fine etcher, particularly in his fantasies of ancient Rome and Egypt. In America the architect Henry van Buren Magonigle (1867-1935) provided a smoother style of watercolour rendering based on the work of Louis Guérin, using large areas of cool colours, often with deep blue skies. This style was followed in England by Cyril Farey and his many imitators. In Farey's meticulous drawings it always looks as if it has just been raining as the streets always reflect the buildings. Farey was particularly good at showing motor traffic and passers-by. In the early twentieth century in England a number of artists, like F L Griggs (1876-1938) (who had in fact been a pupil of Mallows), Muirhead Bone (1876-1953) and Frank Brangwyn (1867-1956), specialized in architectural subjects and their

This attractive sheet of sketches by Bertram Goodhue conveys his preoccupation with details, decorations and a romantic nostalgia for the Middle Ages which dominated his designs until 1914. His most famous building, St Thomas's Church in New York, was a work of collaboration in which Goodhue worked out the structure and the details, incorporating rich ecclesiastical-inspired ornament. He was concerned with handicrafts and workmanship, an influence ultimately derived from Ruskin, and his buildings may be described as Beaux Arts Neo-Gothic, and were generally pleasant, cheerful, comfortable and pretty, but bordering on the sentimental.

In 1914 Goodhue abandoned the Gothic in favour of a more Neo-Classical style. His aesthetic formalism was buttressed by Geoffrey Scott's manifesto of that year which eschewed 'moral expression' and social and ethical undertones. The sensuous but gratuitous pleasure that Goodhue captured in these sketches was also the starting point for his Classical style.

work influenced the way in which architects drew and visualized their buildings. One of the greatest Edwardian perspective artists was Charles Gascoyne (d.1917). His work resembled Farey's but he had a much stronger sense of the dramatic quality of buildings. His drawings for Giles Gilbert Scott's Liverpool Cathedral were particularly fine.

A good renderer, acting in the capacity of 'ghost', could rescue a mediocre design and present it as something passable. In capable hands almost any design could be improved by the manipulation of the composition, lighting effects and the provision of attractive foliage. Even the style of drawing could be an attractive feature in itself and distract attention from the inadequacies of the scheme.

Artist-draughtsmen, like Edward Fricken in New York, Paul Lautrup in Chicago, Mallows and Farey, produced designs in their own right, while others, like Harvey Ellis of Minneapolis, whose projects filled the *American Architect* from 1887 to 1894, interpreted the ideas of others.

This practice of architects working as draughtsmen for others has continued to this day via such formative figures as Hugh Ferris in New York in the 1930s. And it was not just the architects who could not draw who employed them: Ferris, for example, worked for the fine draughtsman Raymond Hood. Today, Steve Oles is a partner in a thriving design practice in the USA, but also produces renderings for the best-known commercial offices such as I M Pei. Perhaps even better known is Helmut Jacoby, who draws in a very individual if rather cold and lifeless style for architects in the United States, Britain and Europe, while carrying on an occasional architectural practice in Wiesbaden, for which his drawings are considerably freer and more charming.

The first generation of renderers, eighty years ago, worked with a speed and accuracy which we might find difficult to believe today. For the last thirty or so years architects have tended to rely on visually more meagre conventions, presenting their schemes through 'geometrical' drawings distinguished by the application of 'mass produced' colour and tonal aids. Such drawings can hardly equal the expressive power of those of the American Bertram Goodhue (1869-1924), for example, but different circumstances and ideologies were at work in their production.

Fin de Siècle: Drawing in Europe

Among the architects whose main work was done in the first part of the twentieth century, it is hard to sort out different movements, and the part played by individuals within them. Although the *Art Nouveau* of the 1890s was an international movement, it had its most important consequences in Germany where a great deal of middle-class house building was in progress. The work of Voysey and Mackintosh, together with that of their contemporary, M H Baillie Scott (1865-1945) was published in magazines, and had considerable effect on the foundation of bodies like the Vienna Secession and the Deutsche Werkbund. In Vienna, Otto Wagner (1841-1918), and his followers Josef Maria Olbrich (1867-1908) and Josef Hoffman (1870-1956) developed a characteristic style of drawing with a sparse outline and flat washes of colour which suited their rather graphic style of architecture. In Germany Peter Behrens (1868-1940), one of the leading figures in the Werkbund (an association of designers and manufacturers), began his career as a painter: he took up architecture after building himself a house in the artistic colony at Darmstadt. Like so many other artists of the time, he moved from *Art Nouveau* to the form of the austere Classical Proto-Modernism. At the same time in Germany there was a movement towards revived Classicism which was mirrored in England in the work of many young architects who rejected the lead of Voysey and Mackintosh in favour of a style more suitable for grandiose public buildings. Among them, the outstanding draughtsman was E A Rickards (1872-1920). He had a natural talent for exuberant late Baroque ornament which he drew with a soft pencil, often filling his margins with caricatures of fashion drawings. His work typifies the stylish but sometimes rather vulgar world of Edwardian London.

Spain enters this history for the first time with the

extraordinary work of Antonio Gaudí (1852-1926) in Barcelona. His is really the reverse of 'paper architecture', being mainly dependent on craft techniques. Gaudí, however, did make elaborate models and drawings. In France there were two figures before 1914 whose work inspired the Modern Movement: Auguste Perret (1874-1954), who worked in close contact with his builders on concrete constructions, and therefore without elaborate drawing, and Tony Garnier (1869-1948), whose project for *Une Ville Industrielle* remained in the form of brilliantly evocative drawings, by which his reputation is preserved. Antonio Sant'Elia (1888-1916), one of the architect members of the Futurist movement, died too young to have built anything, but is remembered for his drawings of parts of an imaginary city, in which the scale is emphasized by exaggerated perspective.

Frank Lloyd Wright

The career of Frank Lloyd Wright (1869-1959) spans so many generations of architects, and is so rich in buildings and drawings, that it stands apart from the careers of the other 'masters of the Modern Movement'. He learnt much from Louis Sullivan, but quickly developed his own style of drawing, a style which was strongly influenced by Japanese prints and employed flat areas of delicate colour. In the early part of Wright's career many of his presentation drawings (the perspectives intended for showing to the client and for publication) were done by Marion Mahoney Griffin, whose husband Walter Burley Griffin worked with Wright for a time. Wright's work became known to a wider circle when a large collection of his designs was published by Ernst Wasmuth in Berlin in 1910. These necessarily lost some of the more delicate colouring, but some were worked up with blocks of solid black shadow, which suited the presentation of buildings like the Robie House and the Unity Temple which was also shown in a five-colour drawing. The one hundred plates, measuring approximately 16 by 25¼ inches, were lithographed in grey or brown ink on either tissue paper or

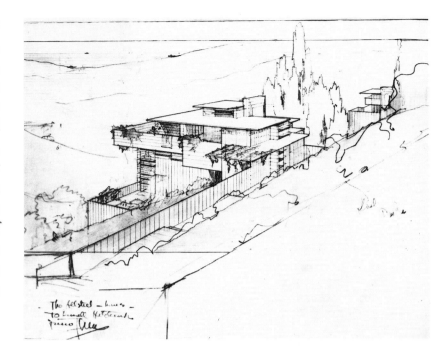

Frank Lloyd Wright experimented with various materials, but was less interested in their different properties than in the formal qualities of mass and volume. In this design for an 'all steel' house he ignored the most obvious use of steel – the structural frame – and used it to form infill panels. This image shows the play of insubstantial planes and lines against abstract solids and voids.

smooth wove eggshell or grey paper. (The most prevalent combination in the portfolio was grey ink on eggshell.) On a very few drawings, a superb extra effect of gold on grey was added by dusting with bronze powder after printing, while one drawing (Lake Street view of the Unity Temple) was printed in five colours in addition to brown line on grey paper. At other times, Wright based his perspectives directly on photographs, and for colouring he frequently used coloured pencils, a technique which has recently returned to popularity, perhaps because, unlike watercolour washes, they can be used effectively on poor-quality paper.

In 1932, when the mechanistic image was reaching its European zenith, Frank Lloyd Wright wrote about his love of the subtleties of coloured pencils: 'The most pleasurable thing I could imagine was that I might go into some shop where fine

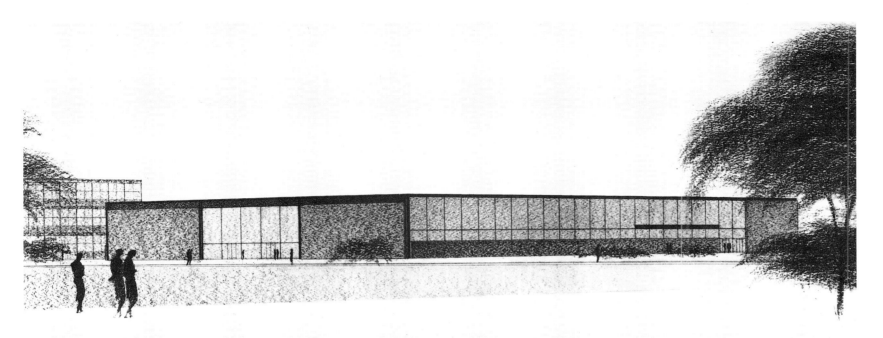

This drawing by Mies van der Rohe (1944) demonstrates his obsession with the formal qualities of pure line and undifferentiated mass, as well as homogeneous space. The mechanical graphic technique suits the qualities of the building, where the characteristics of materials are sublimated and the articulation of elements is severely reduced.

coloured pencils were kept, and gather some of every colour I had ever seen and perhaps some never seen before . . . They are immediately associated with my sense of happiness and have been since childhood'.

The Modern Movement and Expressionism

The history of architecture in the years immediately preceding and following the First World War in Europe is extremely complex, not least because many of the participants sometimes falsified their recollections of what they and others had believed and done. We have already noted the reaction to *Art Nouveau* and the return of a kind of Classical simplicity in the work of Behrens. This was taken up in the work of Behrens' pupils, Walter Gropius (1883-1969), Ludwig Mies van der Rohe (1886-1969), and Charles-Edouard Jeanneret, alias 'Le

Corbusier' (1887-1966), whose work has been seen to dominate the first half of the twentieth century. In their rejection of ornament and acceptance of a 'machine aesthetic' and in their interest in 'functionalism' and the possible uses of new materials, they stand as much at the end of a series of nineteenth-century traditions as at the beginning of new ones.

They were not, on the whole, architects who relied greatly on drawings which were beautiful in themselves. Mies and Gropius had an interest in transparency, achieved with glass, which cannot be properly captured with a single viewpoint and a single effect of light. Realistic representations were in any case unpalatable and Gropius' students at the Bauhaus were encouraged to build models. Mies made use of photomontage, often incorporating photographs of models, in presenting schemes. Le Corbusier's drawings are familiar from the published volumes of his work, some of them being finished in the 'outline' style (although with a more shaky line than his early nineteenth-century precursors). With their simplification of shapes and scale, and the careful choosing of viewpoints, they are as deceptive as the work of the 'renderers' in making attractive buildings which we now

In 1914, at the Werkbund exhibition in Cologne, Paul Scheebart announced that glass architecture would 'bring us a new age'. The architecture of this 'new age' was to be unlike anything before it. Scheebart envisaged an architecture of steel and glass; new constructions were to be cleansed of old forms. He foresaw buildings naturally emerging from the hidden structural logic of new materials of construction. This drawing by Bruno Taut shows how an architecture of this kind would develop in the manner of a crystal, self-generating and self-sustaining. Architectural drawing was seen as the means by which designers would assist the spontaneous generation of new forms.

know from experience would not necessarily be so. In his travel sketches and rough projects Le Corbusier used a thick soft pencil, producing an impression quite at odds with the crispness of his actual work. It is important to appreciate the radical difference between Le Corbusier's concept diagrams – their untutored, spontaneous quality – and his more conventional construction drawings. This split exaggerated the division between the poetic and technical aspects of design.

In the Expressionist movement, which was eventually extinguished by the orthodoxy of Bauhaus-inspired design, there is much more to attract the enthusiast of architectural drawing. The movement was provoked by the unsettled conditions in Germany at the end of the First World War when, as in eighteenth-century revolutionary France, architects used the enforced idleness of social and economic upheaval to dream about the future. The projects of Hans Poelzig (1869-1936), Erich Mendelsohn (1887-1953) and Bruno Taut (1880-1938) are all interesting as pieces of graphic art, irrespective of their architectural content. The buildings were conceived primarily in terms of external volume and internal space, and were often crudely drawn to emphasize their force and massiveness. Mendelsohn's projects use heavy black lines which convey his ideas much more forcefully than the most famous example of his built work in this style, the Einstein Tower at Potsdam, succeeds in doing. Some of Hans Poelzig's most effective drawings are in the outline style, while others are charcoal sketches in which the architectural element is only just recognizable.

The assimilation of architecture into the artistic *avant-garde* also took place in Russia following the Revolution and during the brief flowering of the Constructivist movement, which included architects like Vladimir Tatlin (1885-1953) and Melnikov, whose work stands between the Utopian projects of the German Expressionists and the cool geometry and colours of the Dutch group De Stijl, whose principal architectural examplar was Gerrit Rietveld (1888-1964).

Among the Expressionists is the American draughtsman Hugh Ferriss (see Plates 84 and 85), a master of the use of charcoal in the portrayal of New York skyscrapers which he abstracted into planes of light and shade. In his book *Metropolis of Tomorrow,* published in 1929, he offered dramatic views of the city which in reality was hardly less fantastic. Another master of pencil and charcoal was Eliel Saarinen (1873-1950), a Finn who emigrated to America after making his mark in the Chicago Tribune Tower competition of 1925, for which Gropius and Adolf Loos also produced designs.

Twentieth-Century Drawing

The dominant trends in twentieth-century architecture have been opposed to the production of drawings except for the most utilitarian purposes. Perspectives have been largely replaced by models or axonometrics, and the work of the small number of renderers after the Second World War, such as JDM Harvey and Myerscough Walker, is crude by comparison with earlier work. More recent renderings by Helmut Jacoby, using fine line in a mechanical way, are examples of a considerable but purely graphic talent. These renderings, unfortunately, seem to be the kind of drawings which large commercially oriented practices require. However, not all the architecture of the last fifty years has followed this pattern. Among the early practitioners of Modernism, Alvar Aalto (1898-1976) did a large number of drawings of an intensely personal kind, using a soft pencil on continuous sheets of paper and 'thinking out loud' while searching for solutions to architectural problems. Similarly Louis Kahn (1901-77) did a large number of 'private' drawings, often when travelling, which reflect the changes in styles of painting over the years, but which have the added interest of relating to his architectural work. Kahn's post Second World War drawings are etched so strongly with a black pen that they even tear through the paper. In the 1950s he produced another powerful series of drawings in vibrant, strong colours. The sketch was not so much an adjunct (albeit primary) to the process of building and construction, but a record or graphic embodiment of the architect's creative thought.

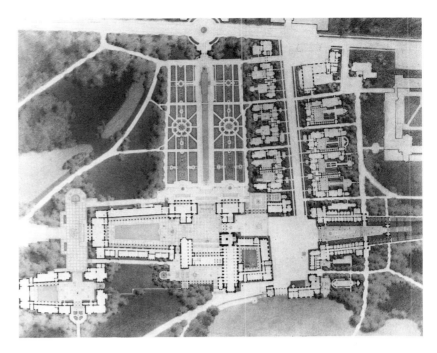

The work of Eliel Saarinen (1873-1950) was highly valued in his own time, and he was invited to leave his native Finland to open a new school of art and architecture in the USA. His plan for the new Cranbrook School, shown here, is indicative of his eclectic approach, both in graphic technique and in the combination of plan arrangements advocated by Camillo Sitte with those of Beaux Arts garden design.

An English architect whose 'private' travel sketches of architecture are now extremely well known is Sir Hugh Casson, and many other architects have produced attractive drawings 'off the record' which have little connection with their architecture.

The above summary might serve to describe architectural drawing fifteen or twenty years ago, but there have been new developments. Disenchantment with the conditions of practice in the competitive world of modern architecture has led a number of architects to concentrate on doing a few things as well as possible by keeping their offices and work on a small scale. They include the Philadelphia practice of Venturi and Rauch and the group known as the New York Five. Their interests include the reintroduction of elements of historical styles, and also the revival of earlier techniques of drawing,

This drawing by James Stirling (1978) poses perceptual difficulties: to grasp its meaning one must take up a point of view beneath the façade. More abstract than perspective and bird's-eye constructions, it is less an image of something seen than a diagram of something thought. The outline graphic technique contributes to its diagrammatic character.

including the dazzle technique which has been used in the Venturi office. The coloured pencils of Frank Lloyd Wright have reappeared in the drawings of Michael Graves and Leon Krier and are now a vital part of the equipment of many architectural students. Since it frequently happens that these architects do not manage to get their work built, their drawings have an added importance in communicating their ideas. At the same time there has been a renewed interest in the history of architecture and of architectural drawing. In recent years exhibitions of architecture have also been extremely popular in France, Italy and the United States.

In America a turning point came with the exhibition of drawings from the École des Beaux Arts at the Museum of Modern Art in 1976. The Beaux Arts, which had been long seen as part of the shady and ignoble past of American architecture, was given academic respectability by the researches of young scholars, and the artistic effect of the drawings displayed was its own justification. A Beaux Arts conference held at the Architectural Association in London in 1978 carried the message to Europe, although senior architects who spoke there, like James Stirling and Colin St John Wilson, could not accept such a dramatic reversal of previously accepted orthodoxies.

More recently still, architectural drawings, both new and old, have been appearing in galleries and salerooms to tempt the collector into new paths. Although some interesting material has emerged and a widespread public interest in architecture is a very healthy phenomenon, there is always the danger that irresponsible dealing will break up collections of documentary value, and that public collections will no longer be able to acquire important drawings.

THE PLATES

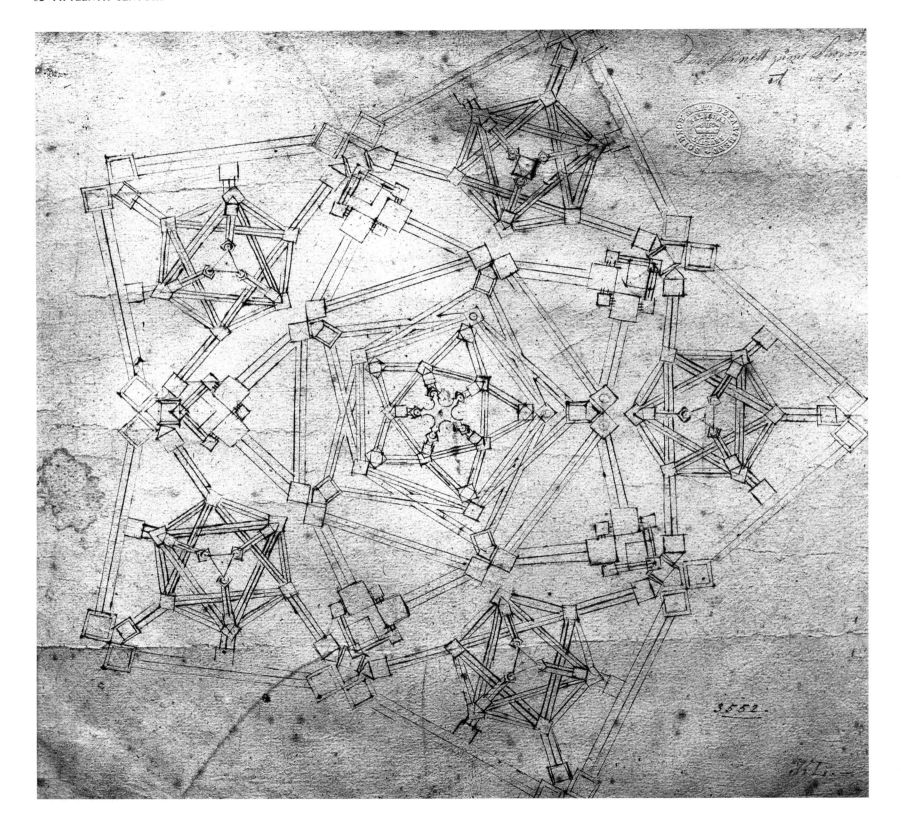

Plate 1

GERMAN ARTIST *(Active Late Fifteenth Century)*

GROUND PLAN FOR A TABERNACLE, ULM CATHEDRAL
Pen and ink on paper, 14¼/14½×12½ in (36/37×32cm)
The Victoria and Albert Museum, London

Long before scaled architectural or 'shop' drawings became essential for the construction of buildings, the medieval architect had developed a system of drawing which appears highly conceptualized but did, nonetheless, serve to direct the activities of the masons' working for him. This drawing, a detail of the middle zone of a much larger project for a tabernacle, was deposited, along with a number of other related drawings, in the cathedral workshop at Ulm. Unfortunately, the project was never carried out.

The masons working from this design, which indicated the architect's intentions in a most summary fashion, translated it into reality, drawing upon centuries of inherited knowledge of the design techniques that had produced the structures around them. The architect, on the other hand, would often produce several versions of the same design project, by manipulating the potential within certain geometric forms, notably the circle, square, triangle and pentagon. He would then select one of these versions to be executed by his team of masons. There was obviously a certain amount of 'play' between the general conception of the project and its execution, but medieval scholars are beginning to realize that the gap is not as wide as previously assumed. This might help to explain why the presence of the architect was so necessary for the workshop, so that he might make the required corrections and adjustments on the spot.

CH

Plate 2

GERMAN ARTIST *(Active Second Half of the Fifteenth Century)*

ELEVATION OF A PORCH ON THE WEST FAÇADE, REGENSBURG CATHEDRAL
Pen and ink on paper, 54×33in (137.1×83.6cm)
Akademie der Bildenden Künste, Vienna

Medieval architects were encouraged, if not contractually obliged, to leave their designs with the large lodges they had headed. These precious drawings, like the numbered templates cut to determine the profiles of architectural members, would be required in the event of any repairs to the fabric. Of course, elevations of the different sections of the cathedral's interior and exterior, such as this view of the porch on the west façade of Regensburg Cathedral, were retained for consultation during the execution of the project. Despite the fact that architectural drawings became much more precise and detailed in the fifteenth and sixteenth centuries, drawings to scale remained quite rare.

CH

Plate 3

GERMAN ARTIST (Active Late Fifteenth Century)

DESIGN FOR THE FAÇADE OF A TOWN HALL
Pen and ink on parchment, 40×15 in (102.4×38.6cm)
Akademie der Bildenden Künste, Vienna

During the medieval period the ground-plan was not as important as the elevation; as one scholar put it: 'the major innovations came not within the ground-plan but from the elevation' (P du Colombier, *Les Chantiers des Cathedrales,* Paris, 1973, p. 87). How would an elevation, such as this one for a town hall, have been used by the mason's shop? Compasses might have been used to enlarge or reduce detail but, as far as we know, even in the late fifteenth century compasses were considered a relatively new invention by the medieval mason. It appears that much of the work was done by eye. The secrets of the masons' trade, which enabled them to work from elevations like this one, were jealously guarded; in 1459 the statutes of Ratisbonne prohibited the transmission of these secrets to anyone outside the guild.

Drawings such as this were invaluable for the transmission of new stylistic information; and they show that medieval architects constantly updated their style. For example, this elevation resembles the façades of the town halls of Goslar and Wesel; and, although this particular project was never executed, it has been postulated that the two buildings were studied in preparation for this project.

CH

Plate 4

*HANS SCHMUTTERMAYER (Active
Late Fifteenth Century)*

*DESIGN FOR A PINNACLE AND
GABLET, FROM THE
FIALENBÜCHLEIN (BOOKLET
ON PINNACLES), c1486*
*Pen and ink on paper, 8⅕×6 in
(20.9×15.2 cm)*
Germanisches Nationalmuseum, Nürnberg

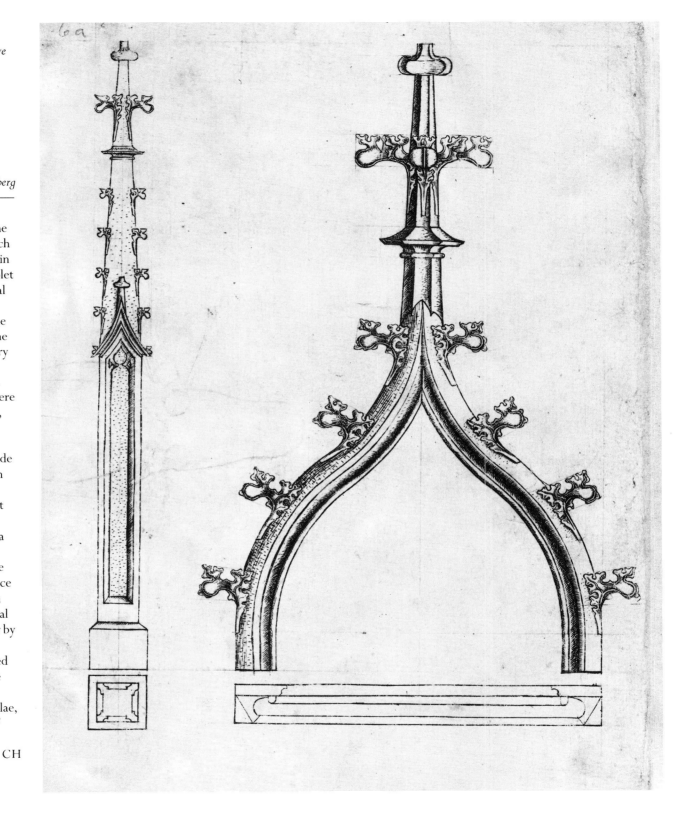

Unlike Renaissance architects
who were concerned with the
theory of architecture, masters such
as Roriczer and Schmuttermayer, in
their booklets on pinnacle and gablet
construction, wrote more practical
'how-to-do-it' guides.

Schmuttermayer mentioned the
art of geometry in his preface to the
Fialenbüchlein, but for him geometry
simply meant a technique of
measurement for measured work.
The trade secrets of the masons were
transmitted verbally for centuries,
and booklets such as this did not
begin to appear until the fifteenth
century, when an attempt was made
to record the valuable information
for subsequent generations of
masons, as the role of the architect
began to change.

This design method was really a
very simple technique of
determining the dimensions of the
parts and whole of the project, once
the modular dimensions had been
established in the basic geometrical
figure. As was stated so succinctly by
one medieval architect: 'Ars sine
scientia nihil est'. What is intended
here is not 'science' in the way we
understand it today but the
application of these simple formulae,
which were based on centuries of
practical building experience.

CH

Plate 5

HANS BÖBLINGER II (fl 1501)

ELEVATION OF THE SPITALKIRCHE, ESSLINGEN
Pen and ink on parchment, 22⅘×25 in
(58.1×63.3cm)
Akademie der Bildenden Künste, Vienna

This drawing of the Spitalkirche in Esslingen was executed by Hans Böblinger II, son of Matthew Böblinger, who was the architect of the church from 1485 until its completion in 1494. It depicts the church (now destroyed) with its exquisite south portal in elaborate detail. Scholars are still uncertain if a drawing of this nature played any special role within the stonemason's workshop. The Böblingers, an important family of German stonemasons, were typical in that they passed on their trade, with all its secrets, for generations. In addition to being a renowned architect, Matthew Böblinger published a booklet on leaf design which is an important document for our understanding of architectural practice in the Gothic period. It demonstrates the architect's concern with forms that might prove useful in the design stage.

This drawing is a reminder that self-portraits of the architect were becoming more common during this period: in the upper section of the roof is a self-portrait of the artist, inheritor of his father's flourishing trade, depicted as a young and elegant dandy gazing out of the window. The inscription on the bottom of the drawing tells us: 'My father Matthew Böblinger erected this building in the hospital of Esslingen. I, Hans Böblinger, have copied it as it stands in the year 1501.'

CH

Plate 6

NÜRNBERG SCHOOL *(Active Early Sixteenth Century)*

DESIGN FOR THE PAINTING OF A FAÇADE (?)
Pen and ink with washes of colour, on linen, 22×16⅗ in (55.7×42.2 cm)
Albertina, Vienna

The purpose of this drawing is unclear to architectural historians, some of whom feel that it was produced as part of a series of illustrations for a legal publication which was never completed. It has also been suggested that it was one of a series of designs for a room in a Hall of Justice. Its connection with a Hall of Justice or legal publication seems certain when we note the guards chatting amongst themselves in the upper storey of the building. Another indication of its original purpose is the small group of Samson rending the jaws of the lion, a familiar theme suggesting the triumph of good over evil.

The fact that the drawing is highly finished means that it would have been suitable for presentation to a prospective client. The Albertina in Vienna possesses several other drawings of this type which may be connected with this project. With the development of a precise theory of optics and mathematics, which led to the theory of linear perspective, the medieval world was left far behind, and a drawing such as this, though only decades after the work of Roriczer and Schmuttermayer, represents an entirely new epoch.

CH

Plate 7

DONATO BRAMANTE (1444–1514)

SKETCH OF RUINS (AND VIEWS OF THE PANTHEON)
Pen/brush and red chalk and brown ink, 10×16⅝ in
(25.2×42.4cm)
Uffizi Gallery, Florence

Twenty years after his death, Bramante was described by the author-architect Sebastiano Serlio as 'the inventor and light of all good architecture, which had been buried until his time'. Serlio's opinion was shared by others: in the sixteenth century Bramante's reputation was unsurpassed. Although he made significant advances in the theory of perspective, his reputation rests principally upon his original and influential achievements in architectural practice. In Milan he made early experiments with perspective illusionism in the interior of one of his churches; in Vigevano he built the Piazza Ducale, one of the first Renaissance 'piazza salons'; and in Rome he built highly original cloisters, gardens, streets, churches, palaces, houses and monuments.

Like numerous Renaissance architects, Bramante practised many arts, and his 'painterly' approach to architectural design and drawing can be seen in his sketches. In this drawing one can see his sensitivity to light and materials, as well as his appreciation of foreshortening in perspective depth. These characteristics differentiate his drawings from those of his contemporaries, who concentrated on size and geometrical form alone.

DL

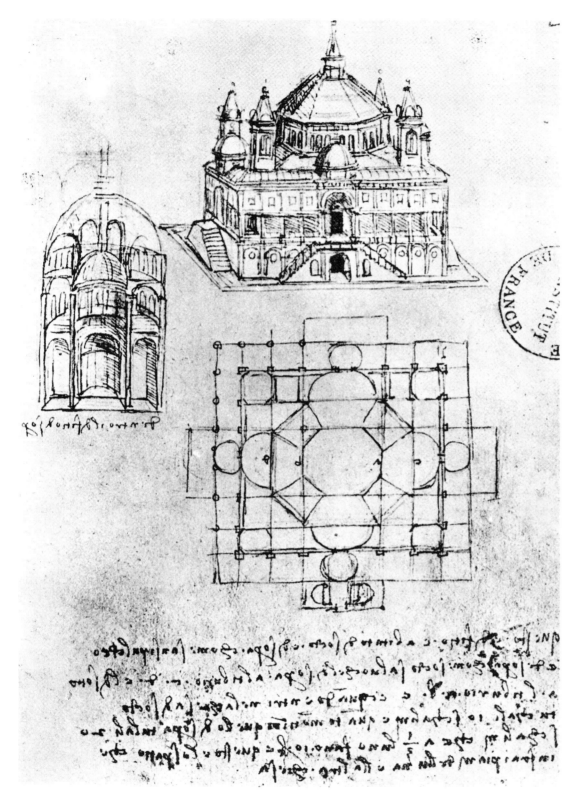

Plate 8

LEONARDO DA VINCI (1452-1519)

PLAN, SECTION AND PERSPECTIVE VIEW OF DOMED STRUCTURE OF SQUARE PLAN WITH PORTICOED FAÇADES
Pen and ink and water colour, 9×6¼in (23×16 cm)
Bibliothèque Nationale, Paris

Leonardo da Vinci's fame in painting, anatomical research and mechanics has partially eclipsed his important contribution to the history of architectural drawing. Leonardo was deeply interested in the problems connected with all kinds of pictorial representation; he executed drawings of the human figure, mechanical devices and buildings. Early in his career he abandoned the 'window perspective' as a means of representation because he found that it could not achieve the optical realism for which he strove. In place of the window perspective he substituted the 'design perspective', otherwise known as the bird's-eye view, an example of which is shown here. From the aerial point of view one can grasp the three-dimensional object as a whole, or as much as a whole as is possible in graphic representation. But the strength of Leonardo's technique is an indication of its weakness; the high and distant vantage point that gives a sense of the whole also reduces the sense of scale. Buildings drawn from above are easily understood as complete objects, but unfortunately they are also difficult to perceive as inhabitable spaces.

DL

Plate 9

GIULIANO DA SANGALLO
(1445-1516)

DETAILS OF THE COLISEUM
Pen, ink and wash, 15½×17⅘in
(39.4×45.2cm)
Vatican Library, Rome

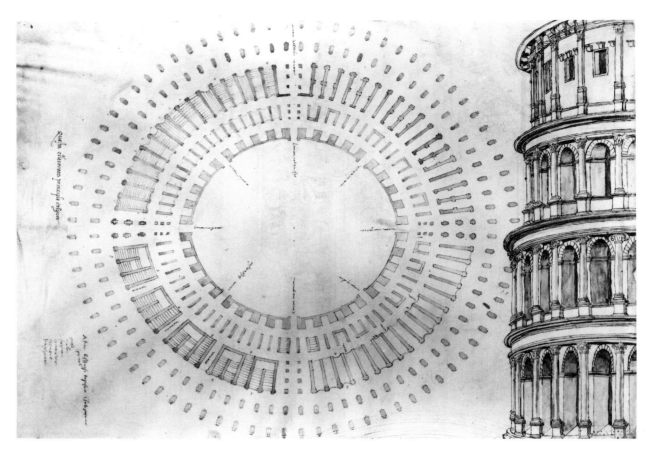

Like all Renaissance architects, Sangallo was deeply interested in the remains of ancient Roman architecture. Together with the ancient descriptions of classical buildings (in texts like those of Vitruvius, Pliny, Strabo and Cicero) the early Renaissance interpretations of ancient monuments were the materials out of which the 'rebirth of antiquity' was fashioned. After training in Florence, Sangallo went to Rome where he worked on various Vatican projects (as a foreman) and began his long and detailed study of ancient monuments. The Coliseum, or Flavian Amphitheatre, second only to the Pantheon in completeness, attracted attention because of its unique use of the Classical Orders. The arches of the first three storeys were separated by engaged columns whose capitals were of the Doric order on the ground floor, the Ionic order on the first floor and the Corinthian order on the second floor. The third-floor wall was adorned with Corinthian pilasters. The idea of superimposing the orders was taken as a key to the problem of designing double- and triple-storey façades, such as those on basilica-type churches. Sangallo's concern for geometry and sizing parts is shown in the care with which he has drawn the plan. His concern with the 'body' or three-dimensional form of the building is shown in the perspective sketch of the exterior.
DL

Plate 10

BALDASSARE PERUZZI
(1481-1536)

INTERIOR OF ST PETER'S, ROME
Pen and ink, 13½×18¼in
(34.5×46.4cm)
Uffizi Gallery, Florence

Of all the remarkable drawings by Peruzzi, this cut-away plan-section perspective sketch of St Peter's is perhaps the most interesting. Although many architects after Peruzzi used this form of representation, no one before him used it. Its virtues are many. Because the drawing shows part of the ground plan it gives an indication of the relative position of the principal elements. The piers shown in horizontal section reproduce their plan forms, but also give an impression of their solidity. The interior under the cupola shows how the vertical members support the vaulting and thus convey the qualities of the whole spatial enclosure. The drawing also shows how the interior would be seen by an observer standing under the great dome. This aspect differentiates it from the bird's-eye views of Leonardo da Vinci, which give an impression of the building as a whole but do not indicate the way it is experienced from within.

The fact that this drawing utilizes differential representational conventions (plan, section, perspective and horizontal section) suggests that Peruzzi was fully aware of the relative strengths and weaknesses of these conventions. His synthesis of drawing types is a remarkable attempt to overcome both the abstract character of orthogonal representations (plans and sections) and the 'subjective' character of perspective representations.

DL

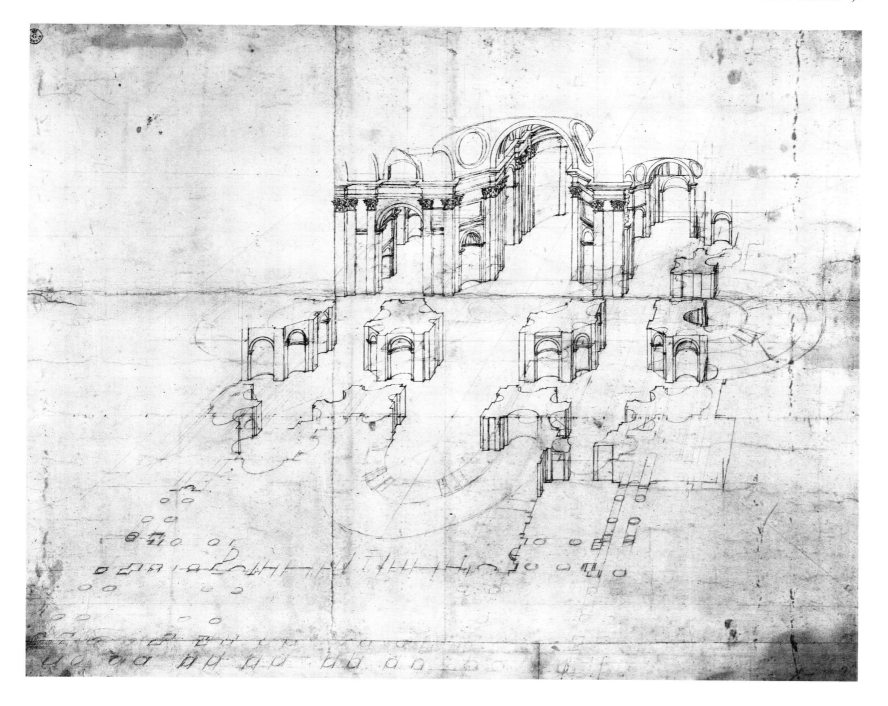

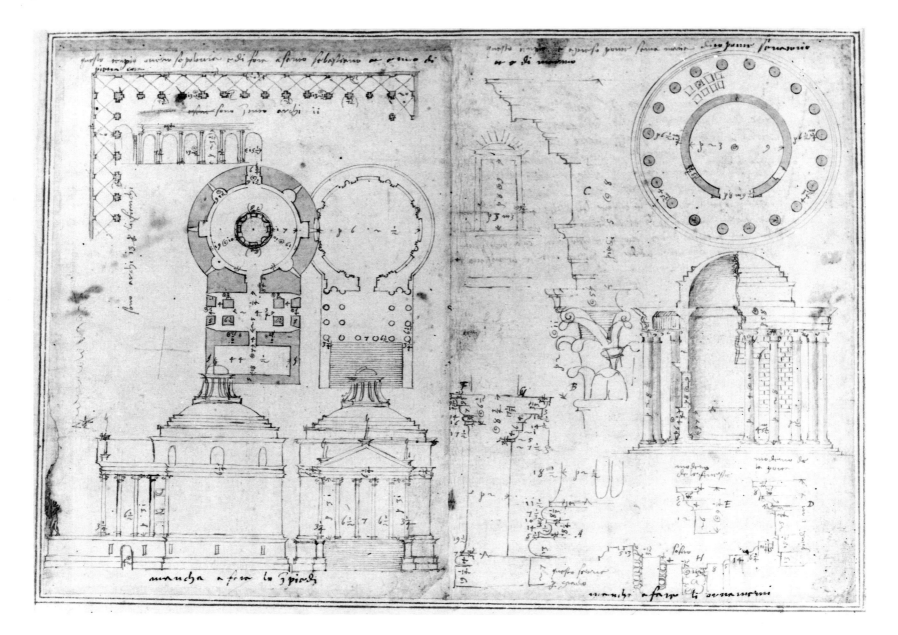

Plate 11

ANDREA PALLADIO (1508-80)

THE TEMPLE OF ROMULUS
OUTSIDE ROME AND THE TEMPLE
OF VESTA
Light sienna ink with grey-brown wash,
11¼×8 in (28.8×20.5 cm)
RIBA Drawings Collection, London

Palladio, born in Padua, made several visits to Rome to study and measure the antique ruins which he regarded as 'the shining and sublime testimony of Roman excellence [*virtu*] and grandeur'. He also collected many drawings and reproductions of the ruins and in 1554 produced two guide books which were taken to be the most authoritative descriptions of antique Roman architecture. Palladio wished to master the principles of Classical architecture and methodically reconstructed many of the ruins which he reproduced in his *Quattro Libri,* (published in 1570) of which this drawing is one. He hoped that these, together with his own designs for buildings, would provide a sound basis for an imaginative evolution of architecture which would combine Palladian rationality with antique authority. The left-hand drawing is a reconstruction of a mausoleum, the Temple of Romulus. All that remained in Palladio's day was the lower vaulted storey (shaded) of a Pantheon-like structure. His reconstruction was derived from several sources and influenced his design for the chapel at the villa of Maser. The drawing on the right is a reconstruction of the Temple of Vesta in Rome. It had lost its entablature and dome which Palladio carefully reinterpreted. His reconstructions reveal his preoccupations with measure, proportion, centralized plans and

temple architecture. His final drawings were always orthogonal to represent the true measurements of the building.

HP

Plate 12

MICHELANGELO BUONARROTI
(1475-1564)

FIRST STUDY FOR THE DOME OF ST
PETER'S
Black pencil on white paper, 9½×10¼ in
(24×26 cm)
Wicar Collection, Musée des Beaux Arts, Lille

Michelangelo's works in architecture were centred in two cities: Florence and Rome. In Florence he was employed by the Medici to design a church façade, a chapel and a library, and there he also designed domestic buildings and fortifications. In Rome he built much more: in addition to various ecclesiastical and domestic works he designed central urban monuments and spaces. His most magnificent works show the integration of painting, sculpture and architecture.

Michelangelo's designs differed from those of his immediate predecessors and contemporaries in so far as they relied very little on existing buildings and abstract canons of beauty. More important than classical models and proportionate ratios was the *idea* of the work. Michelangelo described his art as the embodiment of the *disegno interno,* the formative essence or radical concept of a work. The dome of St Peter's, for example, was first and foremost the concrete embodiment of the idea of the celestial vault. Before considering the proportions of an ancient building such as the Pantheon, Michelangelo struggled with the idea of the Heavens. His numerous sketches

represent various stages in the process of realizing the idea. Obviously, the last stage in this process was the actual building of the dome. Michelangelo's drawings were some of the first to be bought and collected, not because they were more beautiful than the drawings of others but because they were the first to be seen as ingredients of what was then considered to be an almost divine creative process.

DL

Plate 13

RAPHAEL (1483-1520)

THE PANTHEON
Pen and ink on white paper,
11 × 16 in (28×40.7cm)
Uffizi Gallery, Florence

Raphael, the artist who has been called the greatest exponent of High Renaissance Classicism in architecture as well as in painting, believed that the art of drawing buildings could be divided into three parts: drawing plans, elevations and interiors. In respect of drawings of interiors, he rejected those which were views based on a central perspective point because they prohibited the differentiation of lateral volumes, in particular side-chapels in a church. In his own work Raphael found it impossible to avoid the presupposition of a specific or localized viewing place for the observer. But through the use of multiple vanishing points, rather than a single point placed on a line running perpendicular from the picture plane into the depth of the space, he was able to achieve a more fully differentiated image of interior space.

His drawing of the interior of the Pantheon is a good example of this. Because the room is circular in plan no single-point perspective construction could accurately represent its three-dimensionality. To overcome this difficulty Raphael placed the observer in the centre of the space, not in front of or outside it, as is inevitable in single-point perspectives. Perception from within involves moving one's gaze from left to right, regularly looking into the depth of each niche and around the mass of each column. The eye moves from dark to light, into each deep space and back towards the centre, passing from one perspective to another round the whole of the interior. Thus represented, the space is not perceived in a single view (which is, after all, no more than a perspective abstraction of normal perceptual experience) but in a number of views, each simultaneously available to the eye.

Raphael's concern with representational accuracy is also noticeable in his sensitive rendering of light and shade. Unlike previous architects, who were principally interested in line and geometry (Albert's *lineaments*), Raphael was also interested in the corporeal qualities of architectural form – the qualities of materials, textures, solids, transparencies and so on. Raphael distinguished objects in the foreground from those behind by means of shading and shadows, not merely foreshortening and size reduction. In this drawing we see the work of an artist who was not interested in geometries and proportions alone. The abstract construction is there, below the surface, but we also have a representation of the concrete qualities of a space as it is experienced from within.

DL

panteon

Plate 14

TOLOMEI RAINALDI (fl 1580)

*SECTION FOR THE PROPOSED
REBUILDING OF S. LORENZO, MILAN*
*Pencil, ink and wash, 7×9½ in
(17.7×24cm)*
The Victoria and Albert Museum, London

In 1573 the Church of S. Lorenzo, the oldest church in Milan, collapsed. According to a contemporary chronicle, 'the whole of the city wept because the finest building it possessed was lying in ruins and might never be restored'. The fear was groundless, however, because shortly afterwards rebuilding began. The church authorities gave orders that the old foundations could not be altered, so the task was to rebuild the walls and the great twenty-metre dome. A number of local architects joined in competition for the commission, and the job was eventually given to Martino Bassi (1542-91).

The drawing shown here is Rainaldi's proposed section for the church. It seems particularly well suited to representing ideas about structural matters, sizes, proportions and so on. Doubtless these issues were very important in the rebuilding work. The drawing is annotated, the structural integrity of the whole fabric is carefully described, and the cut-away, shaded image looks as if it might have been drawn for or from a scale model.

DL

Plate 15

JAN DE BISSCHOP (1628-71)

STUDIES OF CENTRALIZED TEMPLES
Pen and ink and wash (dimensions unknown)
Victoria and Albert Museum, London

Jan de Bisschop was one of many seventeenth-century northern European artists and architects who travelled to Italy to study both ancient ruins and modern monuments. The exact dates of de Bisschop's stay in Italy are unknown; all that is certain is that he left Amsterdam some time after 1640 and was in Rome in 1655. Many of his topographical drawings survive and most of these demonstrate his skill with perspective techniques, a skill that was common to most Dutch draughtsmen. However, the drawings reproduced here raise other problems. This page of sketches shows de Bisschop struggling with the difficulty of representing the interior of centralized spaces, in this case the interiors of three sacred buildings. Centralized spatial enclosures cannot be accurately represented with conventional one- or two-point perspective constructions.

The inadequacies of perspectives were discovered by early Renaissance architects like Giuliano da Sangallo, Raphael and Peruzzi, whose techniques for overcoming the flattening effect of conventional perspective representations included the multiplication of vanishing points, the cut-away section and the projected plan. All of these techniques are used in these sketches by de Bisschop, but he is not as successful as his Italian predecessors.

DL

Plate 16

INIGO JONES (1573-1652)

*DESIGN FOR A MASQUE:
PROSCENIUM AND SCENE TWO OF*
TIME VINDICATED TO
HIMSELF AND TO HIS
HONOURS, *BY BEN JONSON, 1623*
*Pen and brown ink 14¹⁄₂×18¹⁄₃in
(37.3×46.6cm)*
The Trustees of the Chatsworth Settlement

The central work of Jones was the production of masques for the English court. The masques symbolized the changing culture of the court and were primarily allegorical devices created to demonstrate the higher meanings of politics and power. The unfolding action of the play symbolized the Renaissance beliefs in the nature of kingship and the obligations and prerequisites of royalty. The masques themselves were closely modelled on the theatrical spectacles produced for the Medici Grand Dukes of Florence in the 1580s. The stage sets of the masque were radically different from the Elizabethan stage conventions of the 'theatre in the round'. Jones introduced the proscenium arch and the perspectival backdrop which, of necessity, established an ideal viewing point. Many of the courtiers had to be taught how to 'see' the perspectives. The masques were extraordinarily elaborate and employed complex machinery and lighting effects, rich costumes, and magical scene changes to astonish and transport the audience. Jones was a ruthless plagiarist and collected a vast quarry of images to which he had constant recourse when designing the masques.

HP

Plate 17

INIGO JONES (1573-1652)

*DESIGN FOR THE PRINCE'S
LODGING: NEW MARKET PALACE*
*Pen and wash, 7¹⁄₂×12¹⁄₂in
(19×27.5cm)*
RIBA Drawings Collection, London

At Newmarket Palace, Jones produced what became the prototype for the red-brick, stone-quoined, and hipped-roof cubic house of the seventeenth century in his designs for the Prince's Lodging. The drawing is one of two surviving elevations and shows the 'accepted' astylar design. The central triumphal arch motif was derived from Serlio and Scamozzi, but the high roof and tall windows were revolutionary and prophetic of the English country houses of the Caroline and Williamite periods. The actual building was probably a much more economical version of the one shown in the drawing, but the composition of the façade reveals Jones' preoccupations with symmetry, proportion and harmonic ratios.

Jones followed closely the texts of Alberti, Palladio and Barbaro's commentaries on Vitruvius. He wrote in his notes that 'the boddi of a man well proporsioned is the patern for proportion in building' and that 'Eurythmia or fayr number is gratous aspects in composition of the members'. In his architectural designs Jones followed Palladio's example and Alberti's dictum and drew his buildings orthogonally rather than in perspective to show the true measurements. However, the central axis of his buildings and the symmetry of his façades can be seen to correspond to the central focus of the one-point perspective constructions he used in the stage sets for masques.

HP

Plate 18

JOHN WEBB (1611-72)

*SECTION FOR AN ALCOVE IN THE
KING'S BEDCHAMBER, 1665*
Pen and ink, 11½×17½in
(29.2×44.5cm)
RIBA Drawings Collection, London

During the 1660s, when London was decimated by plague and the Great Fire, John Webb had been working on the project for Greenwich Palace, but his lavish state apartments for Charles II were never executed. The interiors would have been a royal equivalent to the magnificent rooms of Wilton House, designed by Inigo Jones and Webb a decade earlier. This drawing of the King's bedchamber shows the deeply coved ceiling, which would have been elaborately painted, and designs for the gilded plaster decorations. The unique palm-tree columns to the alcove containing the royal bed were inspired by Villalpando's reconstruction of Solomon's Temple. The theme of divine kinship, the free handling of the columns, and the stage-like alcove are all evocative of the masque productions of the Stuart court.

HP

Plate 19

UNKNOWN ARTIST (Seventeenth Century)

PALAZZO DEL SIGR A DORIA, c1632
Pen and ink and wash (dimensions unavailable)
RIBA Drawings Collection, London

A lthough this drawing clearly demonstrates a complete misunderstanding of the differences between orthographic and perspective representational techniques, it indicates an appreciation of light and shade, different materials and the figurative possibilities of surface decoration. The drawing was constructed as an elevation, but distinct elements such as the chimneys, the sides of the cornice and the front steps were drawn in perspective. It is as if the artist was primarily interested in the elements that comprise the frontal plane, but after representing those he felt obliged to give an impression of the building as it might be perceived as a three-dimensional object. This is what makes it something of a hybrid. Nevertheless, much attention has been paid to the different properties of specific materials: stone, stucco, glazing and roof tiles. Similarily, much attention has been paid to the iconography: all the relief sculpture has been drawn with great care. Finally, darker shades have been used to indicate the depth of the windows, and shadows have been used to indicate the size and depth of primary decorative elements – pilasters, string courses, window frames and so on.

DL

Facciata del Palazzo del Sigr Antonio marchese di San Steffano. Doria Marchese de S Steffano —

Plate 20

GIANLORENZO BERNINI
(1598-1680)

SECOND STUDY FOR THE FAÇADE
OF THE LOUVRE
Pen and brown ink with brown wash,
10×19½in, (25.4×50cm)
National Museum of Sweden, Stockholm

In 1664 a number of architects in Rome were invited to submit schemes for the completion of the east façade of the Louvre, and the proposal of Bernini, pre-eminent sculptor and architect of the Roman High Baroque, was preferred. His first design might be summarized as an elliptical, secular St Peter's, complete with colonnade embedded in the centre of the west façade of the Palazzo Barbarini. In response to criticisms, Bernini prepared a total of four designs, in which the façade was progressively flattened, but the second one, reproduced here, is certainly the most curious in regard to the issue of depth. The optical effects of the first scheme focused down from the initial sensation of a fortified cloud to disclose carefully graduated penetrations through layers of framed openings. This, as well as all obvious iconographic considerations, was suppressed in the second scheme in favour of a large, dignified palace which, however, was subjected to a massive perspective distortion. Though perspective exaggeration of curved surfaces was quite common during this period, the specific distortions in this drawing (the base of the central range appears ahead of the extreme wings, the cornice behind) merely

confirm what has happened to the theme of depth in the transition from the first to the second scheme. In the first the viewer was invited to participate in an elaborate stage set, whose iconography was fulfilled as the eye passed the portico, whereas in the second the entire palace has become a purely plastic event. It is as if the draughtsman, seduced by the logic of perspective drawing, had conflated two extremes of architectural consideration: the vast theatrical lens of the St Peter's colonnade and the surface articulation of a column base or moulding.

PC

Scala di palmi 250 Romani

Plate 21

FRANCESCO BORROMINI
(1599–1667)

DESIGN FOR THE FAÇADE OF THE
ORATORIO DEI PHILIPPINI, ROME
Black chalk, 16×13¼in (40.6×33.8 cm)
The Royal Library, Windsor

This early elevation for the Oratorio dei Philippini in Rome resists a purely descriptive commentary. The culture of post-Tridentine Rome included a profound mystical element, which ranged from the militant and aristocratic Society of Jesus to the more purely charitable and humble Congregation of St Philip Neri. Borromini's participation in this atmosphere is commonly mis-represented by stressing the more saturnine aspects of his personality. It is a virtue of the drawing reproduced here that it corrects the impression given by its more popular variant in the Albertina (no. 291) that Borromini's work was simply the expressionist product of an unfortunate psychological condition. In speaking of this façade in *Opus Architectonicum,* Borromini declared, 'I made the figure of a human body with open arms, as if embracing all who enter . . . a chest in the middle, where the two arms join'. The obviousness of this conceit as a simple visual analogy serves to stabilize the more hidden dimensions of the motif. One of these concerns the figurative possibilities in architectural order itself, a legacy of Michelangelo (regarded by Borromini as the 'Prince of Architects'). The drawing registers accurately the overall multiplicity of subtle interactions between the various elements which comprise the façade.

PC

Plate 22

FILIPPO JUVARRA (1678-1736)

STUDY IN THE ITALIAN BAROQUE
Pen and brown ink, grey and brown wash,
8¾×13⅜ in, (22.5×34cm)
The Trustees of the Chatsworth Settlement

Some of the earliest visions of ideal cities occur as stage sets. It is within this tradition of the imagined city being a vessel of a culture's deepest meanings that we should consider the *capriccio* reproduced here. It was executed by the most internationally significant architect of the period, Filippo Juvarra, architect to the King of Sicily. Juvarra also designed for the courts of Madrid, Lisbon and Vienna; and he visited London and Paris. This drawing was one of a collection of architectural fantasies dedicated to Lord Burlington in 1730.

Juvarra's international reputation is worth observing because, unlike that of earlier Italian artists, it was not limited to the court in France.

Secondly, it accounts for the cosmopolitan nature of Juvarra's approach. Thus in the foreground of this image we find a canal from Venice, a series of eighteenth-century classical monuments, and finally a background of 'city texture': a small piazza to the left and an (Italian) Gothic church to the right. A direct product of set design, this fantasy exhibits the contemporary fascination with the coordinated superimposition of two perspective orientations – one frontal and

recessive to the centre, the other oblique and recessive to the edges. This is the standard fare of illusive design, as is the lighting. A dark foreground establishes a spatial *coulisse,* and the spectator peers across the shadow into the illuminated fantasy within. However, the theatric tension with reality is over-attenuated, and the artist appropriates the vastness of his subject by means of a sublimation of meanings to a pictorial spectacle.

PC

Plate 23

SIR CHRISTOPHER WREN
(1632-1723)

FIRST PROJECT ELEVATION FOR
WHITEHALL PALACE, 1669
Pen and wash, 19×25½ in
(48.2×64.7cm)
All Souls College, Oxford

S oon after Sir Christopher Wren was appointed Surveyor General of the King's Works, he was commissioned by Charles II to make plans for a royal palace at Whitehall. Charles II was not the first monarch to undertake such a project: in the 1640s his father, Charles I, had asked Inigo Jones and John Webb to make similar designs, and Wren was urged by Charles II to make use of the ideas of Jones and Webb. Unfortunately, nothing came of this grand scheme.

The drawing shown here is one of Wren's sketch designs for the principal façade. On the left-hand side of the drawing is part of the last bay of the existing Banqueting House, and on the right is half of Wren's double-storey central block. These two major pieces are joined by a gateway to the rear courts.

The drawing serves a number of purposes, and is an accurate representation of the range of issues Wren faced when executing this design. Firstly, it shows the general massing of the building: the frontal planes, drawn in sharp outline, cast shadows on the deeper planes. Secondly, it shows the disposition of primary elements: columns, pilasters, windows, niches, and so on, and therefore the rank of different buildings in the order of the whole palace. Finally, it shows the detailed articulation of the walls: rustication, emblematic reliefs, carving and statues, and therefore the symbolic content of the palace.

DL

Plate 24

CARLO FONTANA (1634-1714)

PERSPECTIVE VIEW OF A CATAFALQUE AND BALDACCHINO IN THE CROSSING, 1707
Pen and grey wash, with traces of chalk,
19×11 in (48.2×28 cm)
Royal Library, Windsor Castle

This catafalque was designed by Fontana in 1707 for the memorial service for Pedro II, King of Portugal, which was held in the Church of S. Antonio de Portoghesi, Rome. This drawing is one of a series which variously attempt to coordinate a number of allegorical and emblematic figures. The symbolic function of the catafalque was elaborate; Fontana had to represent not only the King's portrait, exemplary deeds and Christian virtues, but also the triumph of Christianity, the glory of Portugal and the ideas of death and everlasting life. In this drawing the King's portrait is held by angelic heralds and his famous deeds are shown in relief on the sides of the coffin. At each side of the coffin stand allegorical figures which personify his virtues, and below it – acting as supports – stand images of death. The drapery above the portrait forms a baldacchino (a ceremonial canopy traditionally used to indicate a person or place of special importance) and is hung from a royal crown which supports a globe (representing the Earth) that is surmounted by a cross (the symbol of Christianity). This drawing represents Fontana's way of synthesizing a range of visual symbols. As such it is not so much an imitation of pre-existing forms or figures as it is an embodiment of a highly developed inner concept.

DL

Plate 25

ANTONIO GALLI BIBIENA
(1697-1774)

DESIGN FOR A STAGE SET
Sepia pen and wash, 12×11 in
(30.5×28 cm)
RIBA Drawings Collection, London

This is a characteristic example of the theatrical drawings produced by three generations of the Bibiena family. Altogether there were eight Bibienas, and they dominated the field of theatrical design on the Continent throughout the eighteenth century. It is almost impossible to tell their work apart. The family tradition was begun in 1679 by the brothers Ferdinando and Francesco, who made a reputation as designers of stage sets. Two of Ferdinando's sons, Giuseppe and Antonio, followed in their father's footsteps, as did Francesco's sons and Giuseppe's grandson.

Antonio, Ferdinando's third son, trained as an illusionistic draughtsman under his father before going to Vienna, where he was employed by the Holy Roman Emperor Charles VI for more than twenty years, designing catafalques and opera sets. He returned to Italy in about 1745, settling in Bologna where he became famous for his theatre designs. He was also responsible for designing the city's Teatro Communale. His fantastic architectural set-pieces are notable for their illusion of towering height and infinite spatial vistas, combined with richly Baroque detail derived from Borromini.

JMR

Plate 26

*JOHANN BERNHARD FISCHER
VON ERLACH (1656-1723)*

*SCHEME FOR A GIGANTIC
ROTUNDA SEEN BETWEEN TWO
URNS*
Line drawing in sepia, 11½×16 in
(29.3×41 cm)
Österreichische Nationalbibliothek, Vienna

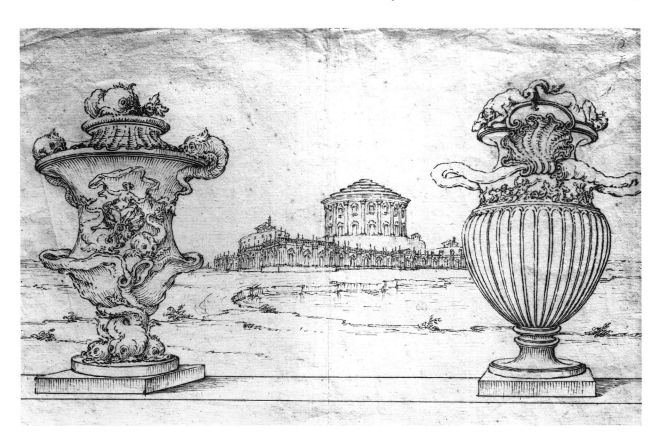

Fischer von Erlach was Austria's
leading Baroque architect. He
began life as a sculptor, and his
interest in elaborate plastic forms is
evident in the two splendid urns seen
in the foreground of this drawing. As
a young man he studied in Rome,
where he was greatly influenced by
the work of Borromini, and it was
while he was there that he turned
from sculpture to architecture.

On his return to Austria in about
1683, he was employed by the
Prince-Archbishop of Salzburg, a
great patron of the arts, and designed
four churches in Salzburg for him
before moving to Vienna, where he
executed most of his major works.
These include the Schönbrunn and
Schwarzenburg Palaces, additions to
the Hofburg, and the dramatic
Karlskirche with its domed rotunda
in the centre, sweeping quadrants,
colonnades and flanking copies of
Trajan's Column in Rome.

Fischer von Erlach was interested
in the dramatic effects of 'movement'
involved in the juxtaposition of a
domed rotunda and concave
colonnades as at the Karlskirche, and
the sketch shown here for an
imaginary building shows his
preoccupation with the same
architectural composition, as well as
his interest in visionary
reconstructions of Classical
buildings.

JMR

Plate 27

GIOVANNI BATTISTA PIRANESI
(1720-78)

THE BASILICA, PAESTUM, 1777
Pen, ink and wash, 18×14 in
(46×36 cm)
Sir John Soane's Museum, London

Piranesi's achievement was to transform the European vision of antiquity. His dramatic and exaggerated studies of archaeological fragments formed one of the major influences on the development of Neo-Classicism and made a great impact on the leading architects of the late eighteenth and early nineteenth centuries. The drama and grandeur of Piranesi's visionary drawings were also an important influence on all later architectural drawings of Classical buildings. The 'emotive devices' he evolved for enhancing the effect of a building were to be copied by a generation of architects and draughtsmen all over Europe.

Piranesi's drawings and engravings of the three Greek temples at Paestum are typical of his work. The temples had been rediscovered in the mid-eighteenth century and were first recorded by a Neapolitan, Count Gazzola, whose drawings were plagiarized by Dumont, while an Englishman, Thomas Major, issued the first detailed survey in 1769. However, it was Piranesi's vision of the monumental grandeur of the temples, published in 1778, which transformed attitudes to them and played a significant role in popularizing Greek Doric as the purest of the architectural Orders.

JMR

Plate 28

GIOVANNI BATTISTA PIRANESI
(1720-78)

IMAGINARY COMPOSITION
Pencil, pen and ink, 29½×21 in
(75×53 cm)
Sir John Soane's Museum, London

Though best known for his archeological studies and *veduti* (views) of Rome, Piranesi was also a master of architectural fantasies. In the 1750s he produced a whole series of perspectives and plans of gigantic and complex structures intended to evoke the genius of ancient Roman architecture. These drawings, whether of tombs, palaces, baths or circuses, are a sort of apotheosis of Roman architecture, far grander than any Roman building can possibly have been. Sarcophagi, obelisks, fountains, rotundas, pediments and colonnades are piled up on top of each other to form a stunning vision of the grandeur of antiquity. This type of fantasy had a great effect on contemporary festival architecture and also on stage design.

JMR

Plate 29

SIR WILLIAM CHAMBERS
(1723–96)

SECTION OF AN UNEXECUTED
DESIGN FOR MARYLEBONE
CHURCH, LONDON, c1772
Pen, ink and wash, 13⅛×17½ in
(33.3×44.4cm)
The Victoria and Albert Museum, London

Chambers began his professional architectural training in J F Blondel's École des Arts in Paris and there picked up the rudiments of French architectural draughtsmanship. He then went to Italy, where he polished his style through personal tuition from the French drawing masters Clérisseau and Péchaux. This beautifully finished sectional drawing is a good example of his Francophile technique with its neat detail and dramatic system for rendering shadows, though this type of sectional drawing is an English convention.

Chambers was first approached to design Marylebone Church in 1770 by the Revd John Harley, and in the course of the next four years he produced two alternative schemes: one for an oval domed church and one for a church with a spire. This section is for the domed version and is obviously inspired by James Gibbs's unexecuted design for an oval church for St Martin-in-the-Fields. In the event St Marylebone Parish Church was not erected till 1818, when a completely different design by Chambers' pupil Thomas Hardwick was chosen.

JMR

Façade Principalle du Pavillon de Bains, Erigée à Paris a L'Hotel de Brancas, Pour Mr le Comte de Lauragnais en l'annè 1768. sur les dessins de Belanger architecte des menûs; Plaisirs du Roy.

Dediè a Monsieur **Williams** Chambers: par son tres humble serviteur Belanger.

Plate 30

FRANÇOIS-JOSEPH BÉLANGER
(1744–1818)

DESIGN FOR THE PRINCIPAL
ELEVATION OF THE PAVILLON DE
BAINS AT THE HÔTEL DE BRANCAS
IN PARIS FOR THE COMTE
DE LAURAGNAIS, 1768
Pen, ink and wash, 16×12¾in
(40.6×32.3cm)
RIBA Drawings Collection, London

Bélanger is famous as the architect employed by the Comte d'Artois for the redecoration of the Château de Maisons and especially for Bagatelle in the Bois de Boulogne in Paris, possibly the most beautiful of all French Neo-Classical *pavillons.* He was one of the leading architects in Paris in the reign of Louis XVI and one of the creators of the French Empire style. He was also responsible for a great many Parisian houses, and this design for a bath house for the Comte de Lauragnais is typical of his work, as well as being a characteristic piece of late-eighteenth-century French draughtsmanship with its strong shadows and careful detail. It is dedicated to Sir William Chambers whom he may have met while Chambers was training in Paris. It is also possible that they may have met in London, since Bélanger had been in England in 1766 to do some work for Lord Shelburne.

JMR

Plate 31

SCHOOL OF ÉTIENNE-LOUIS BOULLÉE (1728–99)

DESIGN FOR A MUSEUM, CALLED TEMPLE DE LA CURIOSITÉ, c 1780s
Pen and ink with blue and brown wash,
13×24½ in (34×62 cm)
Cooper Hewitt Museum of Decorative Arts & Design, New York

The last decades of the eighteenth century in France saw architects obsessed by theoretical projects for gigantic and unrealizable edifices dedicated to some vague social or philosophical purpose, such as combined saltworks and coffee houses, or temples of Reason or cenotaphs. This type of architectural draughtsmanship developed originally under the impetus of the *Prix de Rome* which encouraged students to make beautifully finished designs for ideal structures. But the genre received additional encouragement from the French Revolution which, as well as removing, for a time, many traditional outlets for actual building work, leaving architects with very little to do beyond making drawings, also stimulated a ferment of theoretical ideas for which architecture formed one outlet. Most of these drawings were produced by Étienne-Louis Boullée and his pupils. Boullée was Professor of Architecture at the École Centrale in Paris from 1746, and became a member of the Académie d'Architecture in 1762.

The hallmark of all French theoretical drawings of this type is the gigantic size of the buildings depicted. In this drawing of a building which in form is like any eighteenth-century garden rotunda, the vast scale of the project is indicated by the little human figures which barely reach the top of the bases of the Ionic columns. In fact, this building by a Boullée pupil is less original than the master's own work which makes play with pure geometrical forms unadorned with the more conventional Classical trimmings. Perhaps his best-known scheme is for a cenotaph to Newton in the form of a huge masonry globe (see page 39).

JMR

Plate 32

ROBERT ADAM (1728–92)

SKETCH VIEW OF THE SOUTH OR
GARDEN FRONT OF CULZEAN
CASTLE, AYRSHIRE, c 1776
Watercolour, 13⅕ × 18⅘ in (34 × 48 cm)
Sir John Soane's Museum, London

Perched on a clifftop overlooking
the seas of the Firth of Clyde and
the Arran hills, Culzean Castle,
Ayrshire, is Robert Adam's most
dramatic composition. It
demonstrates that the adoption of
castellated forms allowed the
architect a freedom in design denied
him with Classical formalism.

Robert Adam designed a number
of castles for English clients, but few
were built. It was in Scotland that
there emerged from 1770 onwards a
group of castles culminating in the
compact and powerful Seton Castle,
East Lothian in 1789. There is no
doubt that their combination of Neo-
Classical shapes and castellated
silhouettes is unique in late
eighteenth-century Europe.

At Culzean there are layers of
inspiration. The basic grouping of
ruined arch, viaduct and triple
blocked central mass derives from
Hadrian's Villa which Adam had
sketched while on the Grand Tour.
The Culzean viaduct was to have had
towers along its length but their
superstructures, interrupting the
view to the castle, were omitted.
With a series of bends, an incline and
a walled entrance court, the
approach is oblique, to hold the
castle always in view.

In 1771 the site, a narrow ridge
between a glen and the sea, was filled
by a tower-house which Adam
extended laterally with lower
battlemented wings. Internally, the
processional climax is the circular
drawing-room contained in a
seaward tower. This second building
programme was started in 1787 and
lasted until Adam's death in 1792.

JM

Plate 33

ROBERT ADAM (1728–92)

STUDY OF THE RUINS OF THE
TEMPLE OF JUPITER IN THE
PALACE OF THE EMPEROR
DIOCLETIAN AT SPALATO
Pen and ink with wash, 13 × 24½ in
(34 × 62 cm)
RIBA Drawings Collection, London

Like many other contemporary
artists and architects, Adam
produced numerous capricci in which
fragmented architectural remains are
symbolic of the ruin and decay
effected by time. In his later years,
especially, there are many landscape
studies in which impregnable castles
crouch in mountainous scenery,
whereas earlier drawings evoke his
Classical studies, in this case from the
Temple of Jupiter at Spalato,
Yugoslavia, where he went at the
conclusion of his time in Italy. The
results of the stay at Spalato were
published in 1764 and mark a more
archaeological approach to design.

Adam's investigations at Spalato
were important, since Classical
architectural knowledge, mostly
derived from the remains of temples
and public buildings, lacked details of
Roman domestic architecture. The
substantial remains at Spalato of the
Emperor Diocletian's palace which
incorporated walls, towers, temples,
suites of apartments and galleries as
well as details of the orders, were
utilized at Kedleston, Syon House
and quickly passed into the
repertoire of architecture.

JM

Section of one side of the Staircase.

Plate 34

ROBERT ADAM (1728–92)

*DESIGN FOR A SECTION OF THE
MAIN STAIRCASE FOR HEADFORT
HOUSE, CO. MEATH*
*Ink and coloured wash, 21¼×14½ in
(54×37 cm)*
Sir John Soane's Museum, London

Although Robert Adam never
travelled to Ireland, he received
a number of commissions, of which
Headfort House, Co. Meath was the
most substantial. Headfort was built
between 1762 and 1770, after which
Adam was called in to decorate the
hall, staircase and other rooms.

Staircase designs brought out the
best in Adam, and this one shows
several features of interest. The
cinerarium at the foot may have been
intended as a heating stove, examples
of which are still in existence in the
saloon at Kedleston. The balusters
have a certain thickness which was to
give way to lighter patterns in later
examples, which would sometimes
incorporate brass or bronze with the
ironwork. The intended plasterwork
represents a middle phase, when
Adam had abandoned wall
arabesques in favour of a more severe
style utilizing plaques, often
depicting mythological events, as at
Kedleston and Harewood House. As
was usual in Adam halls and
staircases, the chosen order is the
Doric.

Although critics such as Horace
Walpole sniped at the over-profuse
decoration in Adam's later interiors,
there can be no doubt that in his
middle period, as represented by the
Headfort House proposals, Adam's
restraint would not have found
disfavour with the most sober of
Neo-Classicists.

JM

Plate 35

*ÉTIENNE-LOUIS BOULLÉE
(1728-99)*

*PROJECT FOR A METROPOLITAN
CATHEDRAL, TAKEN ON AXIS
FROM ONE OF THE SYMMETRICAL
ENTRANCES, 1782*
Pen, ink and wash, 13×24⅞ in
(33×63 cm)
RIBA Drawings Collection, London

Boullée was one of the great French Neo-Classical architects who had an enormous influence on the next generation, many of whom studied under him. He is best known for the grandiose imaginary projects which occupied his mind in the latter half of his career, but in the early years, as well as being an architectural teacher, he was responsible for the design of many houses in Paris. It was only later in life that he gave himself up to meditating on vast theoretical projects. Many of these were intended to illustrate his book *Architecture: Essai sur l'Art.* This staggering drawing is one of these and was intended as a church, to be erected in Paris, perhaps in Montmartre, to celebrate the religious mystery of Corpus Christi. But this cruciform Corinthian temple with its almost infinite tunnel-vaulted vistas was more a romantic Classical vision of the nature of God than a practical scheme for a church. Boullée makes this clear in the text accompanying the drawing: 'An edifice for the worship of the Supreme Being! That is indeed a subject that calls for sublime ideas and to which architecture must give character.' Boullée's tricks for indicating huge scale in his drawings were widely copied by his pupils, especially the rendering of shadows and the inclusion of tiny human figures dwarfed to insignificance by the sublime grandeur of the architecture, not to mention the way in which the central vista is made to recede beyond the bounds of vision into clouds of incense, where there may or may not be an altar.

JMR

Plate 36

FLAMINIO INNOCENZO MINOZZI
(1735-1817)

DESIGN FOR THE DECORATION
OF A DOME
Pen, ink and pale blue wash, 14×11 in
(36×28 cm)
RIBA Drawings Collection, London

Minozzi was born in Bologna where he spent the whole of his working life. He became a pupil of Carlo Galli Bibiena, the youngest of the Bibiena dynasty (see note to Plate 25), from whom he acquired the technique of creating exaggerated effects of height in his drawings by clever foreshortening and the dramatic use of light and shade. In this drawing the bright light of the cupola or lantern contrasting with the shadows of the dome is ingeniously rendered.

Minozzi was both a decorator and an architectural painter and his drawings are designs for schemes of *trompe l'oeil* decoration which he actually carried out. He decorated several churches in Bologna and was also responsible for painting the inside of the dome of San Filippo in Forlí in 1780. This drawing is obviously connected with the latter project.

JMR

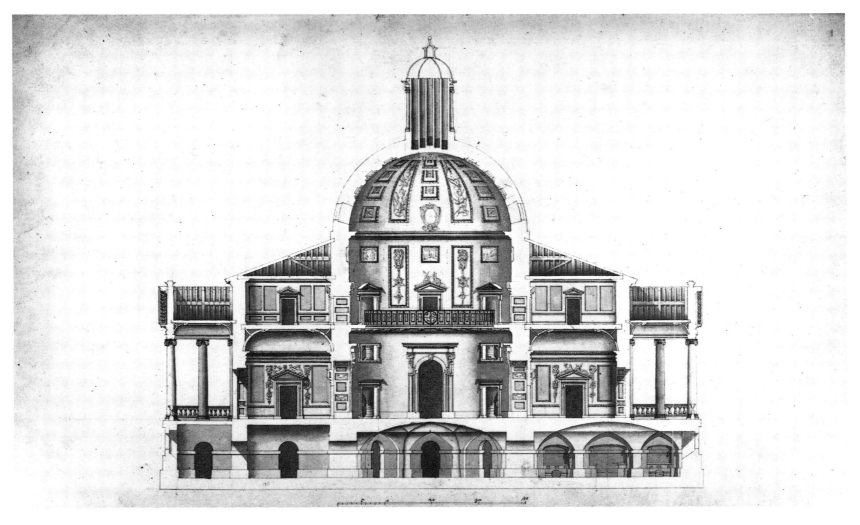

Plate 37

COLEN CAMPBELL (1676-1729)

SECTION THROUGH MEREWORTH
CASTLE, KENT, c1720
Pen, ink and wash, 12¾×18½ in
(32.5×47cm)
RIBA Drawings Collection, London

Campbell made his name as the propagandist of the British Neo-Palladian movement and author of the influential *Vitruvius Britannicus* which helped promote the 'antique simplicity' of Inigo Jones and Palladio at the expense of Wren's Baroque. Campbell was largely responsible for establishing the prototypes from which English Neo-Palladian houses were to develop in the eighteenth century. Among these was the subject of this drawing, Mereworth Castle in Kent, designed by Campbell for the Seventh Earl of Westmorland in the 1720s. It was 'the first and closest of the four English reproductions of Palladio's Villa Capra at Vicenza'. This section shows the house not quite as built. The decoration of the central domed hall, for instance, was changed during its execution. One of the problems with English Classical houses of this type was how to disguise the chimneystacks. Campbell overcame it at Mereworth by putting all the flues in the central cupola, as is clearly indicated here. Campbell was responsible for developing the section drawing as an art form of quality and one which he widely used for his illustrations for *Vitruvius Britannicus.* Such sectional drawings became a popular form among eighteenth-century English architects.

JMR

Plate 38

CHARLES LOUIS CLÉRISSEAU
(1722-1820)

INTERIOR OF A SEPULCHRAL
CHAMBER
Pen, ink and watercolour, 18½×24 in
(47×61 cm)
Sir John Soane's Museum, London

Clérisseau is possibly the best known of French eighteenth-century architectural draughtsmen. He trained originally in Paris under J F Blondel at the Académie d'Architecture, and won the *Prix de Rome* in 1746. In 1749 he arrived in Rome and rapidly made his reputation as a recorder of the Roman scene, turning out a large number of drawings of ruins and assorted antiquities. In the 1750s he was among the pioneers of Neo-Classicism and was closely involved with Robert Adam, for whom he acted as principal draughtsman on the expedition to record the Emperor Diocletian's Palace at Spalato, and he was also employed in a teaching capacity by William Chambers. His reputation reached as far as Russia, and the Empress Catherine the Great acquired a large number of his drawings, though he lost her favour when he designed a huge new palace for Tsarskoe Selo and sent her a bill nearly as huge. His drawings, more topographical watercolours than architectural drawings, are characterized by rich colours and contrasting effects of light, with which he helped to convey the romantic drama of the remains of Classical antiquity.

JMR

Plate 39

BENJAMIN LATROBE (1764–1820)

DETAILS OF THE NORTH WING OF
THE UNITED STATES CAPITOL AT
WASHINGTON, 1817
Pencil, pen and ink, and watercolour,
19×15 in (48.2×38.1 cm)
National Library of Congress, Washington

Latrobe's detail design for the Capitol shows how even working architectural drawings, as opposed to presentation, record and ideal drawings, had developed into an art form by the late eighteenth century. This particular drawing is of interest as it combines three different architectural conventions in one drawing: plan, section and elevation. Latrobe was an international figure, born in Yorkshire and educated in Saxony, who trained as an architect under S P Cockerell in London and spent his active working life in North America. He was the most accomplished Neo-Classical architect in the United States in the late eighteenth century, responsible for the Greek Revival Bank of Pennsylvania in Philadelphia, the elegant Neo-Classical cathedral in Baltimore (derived from James Wyatt's Pantheon), and the enlarged and remodelled form of the Capitol in Washington. The North Wing, the subject of this drawing, was intended for the occupation of the Senate. The ingeniously interlocking plan of the first floor with its oval and apsidal rooms is a good illustration of the Neo-Classical preoccupation with geometry. Latrobe's solution to the problem of the chimneystacks is especially neat: all the flues are incorporated in the lantern of the dome over the central lobby.

JMR

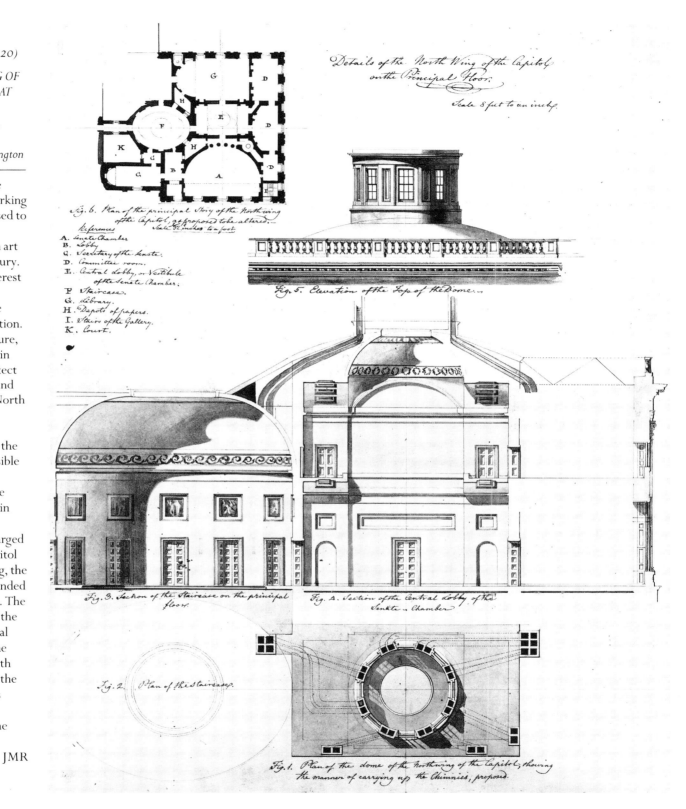

Plate 40

JOSEPH MICHAEL GANDY
(1771-1843)

THE OLD DIVIDEND OR 4%
OFFICE AT THE BANK OF
ENGLAND, 1794
Pen, ink and wash, 26×40½ in
(66×103 cm)
Sir John Soane's Museum, London

Gandy was one of the more interesting English Neo-Classical architects but, being 'odd and impracticable in disposition', he never built up an extensive architectural practice and was mainly employed by Sir John Soane to make elaborate watercolour perspectives of the latter's own architectural designs. Some of the finest of these are his views of Soane's interior of the Bank of England, among the greatest architectural ensembles of the late eighteenth century anywhere in Europe and, alas, destroyed in the 1930s.

Soane's reconstruction of the Bank began in 1791 and continued until 1833. The need for security meant that there could be no windows in the outer walls, and Soane overcame this problem by creating a series of top-lit domed halls with fireproof vaults built out of hollow cones. The Old Dividend Office, designed in 1794, was one of the finest of the Soane interiors with its segmental arches, lanterns embellished with caryatids derived from the Erectheum, and idiosyncratic Soane decoration of incised lines, Greek fret and reeded mouldings. The decoration was not executed exactly as shown in this drawing; the diagonal coffering, for instance, was omitted to create a smoother and more austere effect.

JMR

Plate 41

JOSEPH MICHAEL GANDY
(1771-1843)

PERSPECTIVE OF THE BANK OF
ENGLAND AS A RUIN
Watercolour, 35½×21¼in
(90×54cm)
Sir John Soane's Museum, London

This extraordinary Neo-Classical fantasy, showing Soane's Bank of England as it might appear in a thousand years' time, overrun with vegetation and a gang of New Zealanders camping in the ruins, is illustrative of Gandy's romantic imagination. It is this type of morbid fantasy that led Sir John Summerson to dub him 'the frustrated Wordsworth of English architecture'. Today Gandy is best known as a painter of architectural fantasies, largely because he found it impossible to get commissions for real buildings. His inability to express his ideas in bricks and mortar is a real loss to British architecture, for he was among the most accomplished designers of his generation.

Originally trained at the Royal Academy Schools, Gandy travelled in Italy for three years from 1794-7 and won a medal from the Academy of St Luke for a design for a triumphal arch. In all his work he was inspired by a romantic vision akin to that of the poets and painters of his time. Much of the effect of this watercolour comes from the dramatic chiaroscuro of the architecture, lit by the flames from the bonfire in the rotunda, and the stormy sunset against which the ruins are silhouetted.

JMR

Plate 42

JOSEPH MICHAEL GANDY
(1771-1843)

*A COMPOSITION OF VARIOUS
DESIGNS EXECUTED BY SIR
JOHN SOANE, 1780-1815*
*Watercolour, 28½×51 in
(72×130cm)*
Sir John Soane's Museum, London

This drawing is both a record and a tribute. It shows the major works of Sir John Soane executed in the thirty-five years between 1780 and 1815 as if they were architectural models stacked up in one of the rooms of the architect's own house in Lincoln's Inn Fields. All the buildings are identifiable, though not all of them still exist. At the top, the largest building is the Bank of England seen from the north, with its subtly articulated screen wall with two pedimental entrances and the dramatic Corinthian corner feature derived from the Temple of Vesta at Tivoli. To the left is the façade of Soane's country house at Pitzhanger Manor, Ealing, based on a Roman triumphal arch. To the right is the Mausoleum from the Dulwich Picture Gallery with its idiosyncratic arrangement of the 'Neo-Classical furniture of death'. In the left foreground, partly veiled by black drapery, can be seen the Soane family tomb in St Pancras churchyard (a design which inspired the form of Sir Giles Scott's telephone kiosks) and on the entablature of the beam just under the dome can be espied some of Soane's smaller garden buildings, including the water-house at Wimpole (demolished) and the farmhouse at Butterton in Staffordshire, with a sarcophagus on top of its chimney-stack.

Like many English architects of his generation, Soane was responsible for a series of ingenious designs for model farm buildings and other subsidiary estate buildings. These little compositions are among the most ingenious of English Neo-Classical designs. Because the inhabitants (cows and sheep) were not in a position to object, it is often in these little buildings that the more *outré* Neo-Classical theories were carried into effect rather than in more conventional designs for country houses, churches or public buildings.

JMR

INTÉRIEUR DE LA NOUVELLE SALLE DE COMÉDIE FRANÇAISE DE L'ANCIEN PR

Plate 43

CHARLES DE WAILLY (1730-98)

SECTION FOR LA COMÉDIE FRANÇAISE, 1776
Ink wash and bistre, 24×37 in (61×93 cm)
Musée Carnavalet, Paris

The section of the new theatre for the Comédie Française, now the Théâtre de L'Odéon in Paris, was exhibited in 1781, a year before the completion of the building to a slightly modified design. Marie-Joseph Peyre (1739-85), author of the influential *Oeuvres d'Architecture* and whose taste was for Roman grandeur, collaborated with Charles de Wailly who had been a fellow student in Rome, and whose inclination was more theatrical and decorative. Both had been profoundly affected by Piranesi, as had so many other French architects in the second half of the eighteenth century. De Wailly was responsible for a splendid set of drawings of the proposed theatre which were prepared for public exhibition, showing the severe outlines of the building brought to life by the play of light and the activities of figures in the street and inside the theatre. De Wailly also devised the delicate blue and white auditorium which at the opening was said to be so unflattering to the ladies' complexions.

The building embodied several novelties: seating in the pit; continuous uninterrupted galleries on iron supports; and the unity of stage and auditorium within a single circle. De Wailly was determined to enforce this effect by having columns on stage, which he claimed would enhance the grandeur of moments like the throne-room scene in Voltaire's *Semiramis,* which is probably the play shown in the drawing, but he was overruled and caryatids were substituted. It was a period when architects loved free-standing columns, but their loss on stage is made up by the magnificence of the portico and the staircase halls, which were only surpassed by Victor Louis's contemporary theatre at Bordeaux (regarded as the model for all theatres for more than a century).

This drawing shows the architect's preferred version of the design. Its imaginative realism takes the spectator right into the building by the Renaissance device of a section combined with an interior perspective, so that the effect is like a half-opened doll's house. The light floods into the auditorium and foyer, contrasting with the darkly cavernous roof-space. Although none of the original interiors survives at the Odéon, this drawing enables us to circulate in what must have been an architectural and decorative *tour de force,* and marks a new departure in the drawing's ability to suggest the actual experience of moving through a sequence of spaces in a building.

AP

Plate 44

SIR ROBERT SMIRKE (1780-1867)

PERSPECTIVE THROUGH ONE
OF THE ENTRANCE ARCHWAYS
OF HYDE PARK, 1797
*Pen and watercolour on card, 14×20½in
(35.5×52.5 cm)*
RIBA Drawings Collection, London

S mirke was a talented draughtsman who had displayed an
inclination towards drawing from his
earliest youth. He improved his
technique at the Royal Academy
Schools, where he won both the
silver and gold medals, and then
embarked on an intrepid programme
of recording most of the Ancient
Greek buildings in the bandit-
infested Morea. He was equally
competent as a master of the Greek
and Gothic styles and is best known
for the British Museum, a coolly
perfect masterpiece.

Various proposals for improving
the entrance to London from the
west at Hyde Park Corner had
occupied the thoughts of generations
of architects from the mid-
eighteenth century onwards, and
received a special impetus from
George IV's programme of
Metropolitan Improvements in the
early nineteenth century. Most of
these schemes involved various
dispositions of triumphal arches, and
the scheme eventually executed, to
the design of Decimus Burton,
comprised an Ionic screen and a
triumphal arch. Smirke's project,
however, was for a dramatic urban
square surrounded by three-storey
residential buildings and entered
through semi-circular arches
reminiscent of the approach through
the General Staff Building to the
Winter Palace in St Petersburg.
Much of the impact of Smirke's
drawing comes from his contrasts of
brightly lit surfaces and dark
shadows.

JMR

Plate 45

THOMAS HAMILTON (1784-1858)

THE ROYAL HIGH SCHOOL,
CALTON HILL, EDINBURGH, c1848
Watercolour, 30×53 in (76×135 cm)
The Royal Scottish Academy, Edinburgh

Few architectural drawings manage to convey so dramatic an impression of the cataclysms of history as this evocation of the acropolis of the 'Athens of the North'. In the High School, Doric is used with a rare sense of drama, in response to the effects of light, shade and movement on the picturesque volcanic outcrop on which the school is sited, amidst other Grecian buildings including a reproduction of the Choragic Monument of Lysicrates (Burns Monument) in the foreground and an unfinished Parthenon above. Hamilton enhances the romantic and visionary effect by depicting the buildings against a dark and stormy sky.

Hamilton was among the leading Greek Revival architects in Scotland in the early nineteenth century, and his design for the High School is a major monument, admirably composed and detailed. It is derived from the Theseion. Hamilton was noted at the time for the high quality of his watercolour sketches for his various architectural proposals, and won a gold medal at the Paris International Exhibition of 1851.

JMR

Plate 46

*KARL FRIEDRICH SCHINKEL
(1781-1841)*

*PERSPECTIVE VIEW OF THE
COURTYARD AND PERISTYLE
GARDEN AT ORIANDA IN THE
CRIMEA*
Pen, black ink and watercolour, 17½×19in
(44.6×48.2cm)
Staatliche Museen, Berlin

Schinkel was the leading German Neo-Classical architect of the early nineteenth century, and under him Prussian architecture was raised to European importance. He trained under David Gilly, who had established an architectural academy on the French model in Berlin, before spending three years in Italy. In the years immediately following his return to Berlin in 1805, he was more active as a painter in the manner of Caspar David Friedrich than as an architect, but after 1815, and Prussia's recovery from the Napoleonic Wars, he made his name with a series of majestic public buildings. These were the Barracks of the Palace Guard, the Royal Theatre and, above all, the Altes Museum which, together with St George's Hall in Liverpool, can claim to be the finest Greek Revival building in Europe.

Schinkel, however, was not a strict Revivalist. His buildings, like his paintings, are strongly imbued with a romantic streak and cleverly related to their landscape setting. This is particularly true of the villas and palaces built for the Prussian royal family in the 1820s and 1830s. Orianda was perhaps the most fanciful of these. It was a romantic re-creation of an antique villa intended for the shores of the Black Sea. This drawing shows the pool in the peristyle garden flanked by statues of different wild animals and with a brightly painted colonnade. Rich polychrome decoration formed an important ingredient of early nineteenth-century Neo-Classical architecture.

JMR

Plate 47

*KARL FRIEDRICH SCHINKEL
(1781-1841)*

*VIEW OF THE CARYATID PORCH,
ORIANDA, CRIMEA*
Pen, black ink and watercolour,
19×19¼in (48.2×48.9cm)
Staatliche Museen, Berlin

Orianda was designed for Princess Charlotte of Prussia who married Tsar Nicholas I. She suffered from ill health and it was hoped that the climate on the Black Sea in the Crimea would be more congenial than that of St Petersburg. The villa was planned to stand right on the edge of the water, as can be seen in this view of the landing stage and the caryatid porch. This façade was made up of elements derived from the Erectheum in Athens but combined in an original way. The Ionic columns with anthemion necks based on the Erectheum portico were used by Schinkel to form symmetrical bows flanking the central caryatid portico. Schinkel's drawing, with its sharp shadows, conveys the bright light of the Crimea, and his painting of the masonry gives it a romantic, weathered look.

JMR

Plate 48

*KARL FRIEDRICH SCHINKEL
(1781-1841)*

*CLASSICAL STAGE SET WITH
A DORIC TEMPLE*
*Watercolour over pencil, 15 1/16 × 20 1/4 in
(38 × 51 cm)*
The Minneapolis Institute of Arts, Minnesota

As well as architectural designs and landscape paintings, Schinkel made a large number of stage designs and 'perspective-optical pictures' for panoramas and dioramas. Their free technique and broader treatment contrast with the more precise and linear quality of his straightforward architectural designs. His theatre drawings are notable for their monumental scale, dramatic lighting and imaginative use of archaeological features. Like most Neo-Classical drawings of this type, the treatment and spirit derive ultimately from Piranesi. The squat Ionic temple in the foreground, for instance, recalls Piranesi's drawings of the Greek temples at Paestum (see Plate 27). Schinkel had a lifelong fascination for the theatre and his interest was probably stimulated by the theatre designs of Friedrich Gilly. He produced the stage décor for over thirty productions in the royal theatres of Berlin, and his drawings in this field are considered to be the climax in the development of Classicist theatre decoration.

JMR

Plate 49

CHARLES ROBERT COCKERELL
(1788-1863)

PERSPECTIVE FOR THE ROYAL
EXCHANGE, LONDON, 1840
Pen, pencil and sepia wash, 27×50 in
(68.6×127cm)
RIBA Drawings Collection, London

Cockerell spent several years abroad and became passionately interested in Greek antiquities. He also developed a great admiration for Wren, and this resulted in a highly original style in which Renaissance was mingled with Classical in a grand yet disciplined way.

Cockerell's magnificent design for the Royal Exchange was never built. The competition for a new building, following the burning of the old Exchange, was corruptly managed and won by Sir William Tite. This building would have been Cockerell's finest: it is a rich and subtle combination of elements from the Antique and the Renaissance. This grand and powerful façade, which develops Cockerell's favourite triumphal arch theme, would have led into a top-lit courtyard. Before he became a fastidious Neo-Classical architect, Cockerell had wanted to be a painter, and he was certainly one of the greatest British architectural perspectivists. As with many nineteenth-century perspectives, this very precise and realistic watercolour owes much to the English topographical tradition in painting. Cockerell's most celebrated drawing was one of all of Wren's buildings grouped together in an imaginary combination, but this perspective is one of his best. The

sculptural richness and the monumentality of the building are palpable, and it seems perfectly at home in the bustling city streets. Cockerell drew both people and the surrounding buildings with equal realism and precision. To the right is Cornhill, to the left Threadneedle Street with the façade of Soane's Bank of England (see Plate 40) and, behind, the tower of Wren's St Bartholemew's-by-the-Exchange. The following year this was taken down and replaced by Cockerell's Sun Life Assurance Office, now itself destroyed. This subtly toned drawing shows us exactly what London could and should have had.

GS

Plate 50

LEO VON KLENZE (1784-1864)

POLYCHROME GARDEN TEMPLE IN THE
ROYAL PARK, MUNICH, 1836
Pen and watercolour, 26½×19½in (67.5×49.5cm)
RIBA Drawings Collection, London

Under King Ludwig I, Leo von Klenze was the architect principally responsible for the creation of modern Munich, for which he designed a series of public buildings, some in a Neo-Classical manner and others closely inspired by Renaissance prototypes. A meticulous draughtsman, Klenze had studied Greek and Roman architecture and, like other Neo-Classical architects of his generation, was interested in the use of colour by the ancient Greeks on their buildings. He was the rival of the Frenchman J-L Hittorff in publishing this research on Antique polychromy, and was able to make practical use of his knowledge of architectural colour on several of his buildings in Munich. This Greek Revival garden temple is coloured in the manner he believed was practised in Classical Greece.

GS

Plate 51

HENRI LABROUSTE (1801-75)

DETAIL OF THE ELEVATION OF LA
BIBLIOTHÈQUE STE-GENEVIÈVE, PARIS, c1848
Pen and wash, 27×20½in (68×51cm)
Bibliothèque Nationale, Paris

Labrouste's library, with its extensive use of iron construction, was a revolutionary building. A winner of the Grand Prix, Labrouste had trained at the École des Beaux Arts, which is evident both from his rational approach to planning and construction and in the meticulous precision and elegance of his drawings. The façade of the Bibliothèque, which stands next to Soufflot's Panthéon, was based on Alberti's Church of S. Francesco at Rimini and has delicate ornament in low relief. The principal ornament, however, is the inscribed names of 810 authors, designed to be read, so that the purpose of the building is immediately apparent.

GS

MOI | RACINE
RIT | BOILEAU
NNE | CORNEILLE
IRE | MOLIERE
LIN | ROLIN
INE | RACINE

SENEQUE | MOLIERE | VOLTAIRE
PASCAL | CUVIER | POTHIER
POTHIER | ARIOSTE | OVIDE
BUFFON | HORACE | VIRGILE
VOLTAIRE | HOMERE | CICERON
MONTAI | ABCD | TACITE

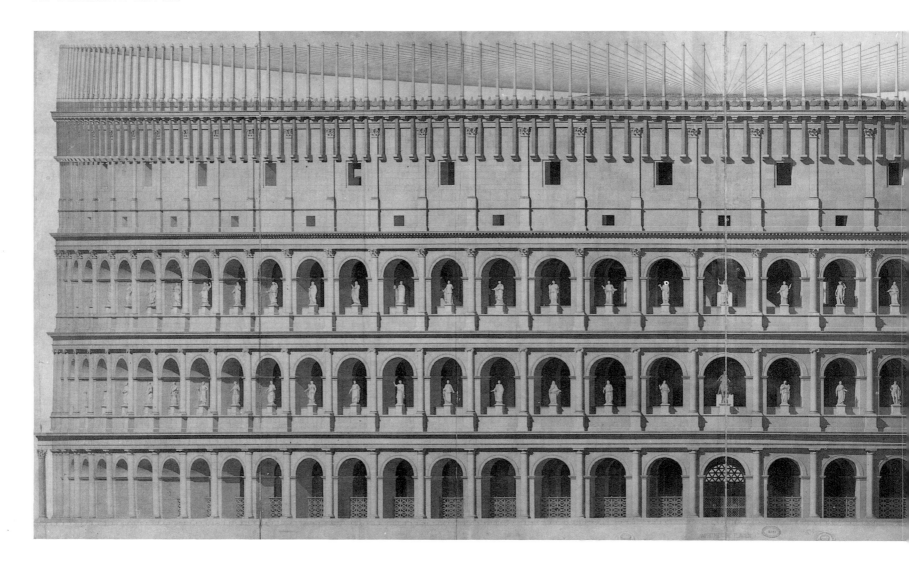

Plate 52

LOUIS DUC (1802-79)

*RECONSTRUCTION OF THE
COLOSSEUM, ROME, 1829*
Grey wash (dimensions unavailable)
École Nationale Supérieure des Beaux
Arts, Paris

Duc was trained at the École des Beaux Arts and won the *Grand Prix* in 1825. A reconstruction of the original appearance of the Colosseum was a typical Beaux Arts exercise, as the curriculum was dominated by the authority of pure Classical architecture. The elevation of the curving exterior was particularly difficult to do, as all the shadows in the rendering had to be indicated with their changing projections. Previous *pensionnaires,* under the influence of Labrouste, had emphasized the structural resolution and spatial variety of the Colosseum façade. Duc, however, focused on the surface of the building, rendering the deep spaces in dark shadows. Duc placed strong emphasis on the detailing of the different orders, but he argued that buildings such as the Colosseum were not decorated as elaborately as other types, such as temples. Accordingly, in his reconstruction the orders are represented with reduced decoration and simple lines. Moreover, structural techniques are not indicated, and differences between various surface materials (such as different marbles, timber and brick) are not shown. The simplicity of his figures exaggerates the sense of precision and mechanical exactitude in Duc's drawings.

It is obvious that Duc, like many Beaux Arts students, was less interested in the iconography or representational content of ancient buildings than the formal or pictorial qualities. In the last decades of the nineteenth century, well after Duc executed this drawing, students considered sophisticated graphic constructions and pictorial techniques as ends rather than means. Nevertheless, Duc's drawings represent the high standards of draughtsmanship maintained at the École. His later buildings, such as the enlargement of the Palais de Justice carried out under Napoleon III, have an ordered approach to planning and construction combined with an intelligent development of tradition.

GS & DL

Plate 53

*ROBERT LOUIS ROUMIEU
(1814-77) AND ALEXANDER DICK
GOUGH (1804-71)*

*INTERIOR PERSPECTIVE FOR A
CHURCH IN HIGHBURY, LONDON,
c 1840*
*Pen, ink and wash, 11⅘×16½in
(30×42cm)*
RIBA Drawings Collection, London

This church was never built. Most of the ecclesiastical work of Roumieu and Gough, who were in partnership from 1836 until 1848, was in a rather mean Gothic style, but this building was to be in a pure Neo-Classical manner with trabeation rather than arched or vaulted construction. With its galleries and prominent central pulpit – which suggests that this might be a Nonconformist place of worship – the design shows absolutely no recognition of the Gothic ideas of Pugin and the Ecclesiologists, and is in complete contrast to Plate 54, in drawing style as well as content.

Longitudinal interior views of churches, taken from a viewpoint on axis, were common in the early nineteenth century. The slight naïve stiffness and coldness of the sharply and finely delineated architectural drawing is greatly relieved by the warmth of the impressionistic human figures, which were almost certainly drawn and painted in by another, unknown hand.

GS

Plate 54

*AUGUSTUS WELBY NORTHMORE
PUGIN (1812-52)*

*BIRD'S-EYE VIEW OF GARENDON
HALL, LEICESTERSHIRE, 1841*
Pen and ink, 7¼×8½in (18.5×22cm)
RIBA Drawings Collection, London

This design was prepared for Ambrose Lisle Philips, a Catholic convert who was one of Pugin's patrons. The project to replace a Palladian house with this moated collegiate manor was probably not wholly serious; rather, it is an ideal design, recalling the medieval world with which Pugin was obsessed. Pugin often employed the archaic 'bird's-eye view' of seventeenth-century prints and he modelled his rather rapid and sketchy style of pen-draughtsmanship on Dürer and Hollar. Such a drawing was prepared as a deliberate reaction to the sophisticated architectural draughtsmanship employed by the Classical architects of the time, such as Cockerell, whom Pugin despised.

GS

Plate 55

HARVEY LONSDALE ELMES
(1814-47)

PERSPECTIVE OF ST GEORGE'S
HALL, LIVERPOOL, c 1840
Pencil and watercolour, 16¼×21¼in
(41.3×54cm)
RIBA Drawings Collection, London

St George's Hall is one of the finest buildings of its date anywhere in Europe, and its powerful massing and Roman grandeur are well conveyed by Elmes's watercolour perspective sketch. Such a drawing shows how the English tradition of draughtsmanship was able to convey the full three-dimensional impact of a building. At a a very young age, Elmes had won the competitions for a concert hall and a new assize court and had submitted fine perspectives for both. The two buildings were eventually combined into this one design, which has an assured Neo-Classical monumentality. Elmes died young, of consumption, before it was finished, and the building was completed by C R Cockerell.

GS

Plate 56

PHILIP CHARLES HARDWICK
(1822-92)

*INTERIOR PERSPECTIVE OF THE
GREAT HALL, EUSTON STATION,
LONDON, c1849*
*Sepia pen and watercolour, 28½×24in
(72.5×61cm)*
RIBA Drawings Collection, London

The opening of the London & Birmingham Railway and the triumph of engineering was first celebrated by the 'Euston Arch', the Doric propylaeum designed by the elder Hardwick in 1836. For the station's booking hall, the younger Hardwick designed something more Renaissance in inspiration, with a grand staircase leading up to the *piano nobile* and the door of the Shareholders' Meeting Room. The murals above the iron gallery were never executed. Hardwick's interior perspective, exhibited at the Royal Academy in 1849, well conveys the room's magnificence, and the booking hall remained the grandest interior in any British station, until it was destroyed by British Railways in 1962.

GS

Plate 57

*EUGÈNE-EMMANUEL VIOLLET-LE-DUC
(1814-79)*

*DESIGN FOR THE RESTORATION OF
CARCASSONNE, FRANCE, 1853*
Watercolour, 25×38⅜ in (63.5×97.5 cm)
*Centre de Recherches sur les Monuments
Historiques, Paris*

Viollet-le-Duc was the principal nineteenth-century restorer of French medieval buildings, and his restoration of the thirteenth-century walled city of Carcassonne was so ruthless and complete that the result is virtually a new piece of architecture. Viollet-le-Duc believed that he was restoring what might have been in its original style, even if there was not always evidence that this was so. This drawing shows his design for the walls of the city at the side of the descent from the barbican.

Viollet-le-Duc was a fine draughtsman and watercolourist who executed all the illustrations in his several books on architecture. Unlike English Gothicists such as William Burges (who restored Cardiff Castle), Viollet-le-Duc was trained at the École des Beaux Arts, and his drawings have a precision and a Classical character lacking in English work.

The illustrations for his most important books, the *Dictionnaire raisonné de l'architecture française du XIme au XVIme siècle* (1854-68) and the *Entretiens sur l'architecture* (1863-72), were steel engravings, and their hard, linear quality makes them very different from the softer and more textured woodcuts used in English books of the period. Similarly, Viollet-le-Duc's executed buildings have a certain hardness of texture and mechanical dullness very different from English Gothic Revival work. His drawings of Carcassonne are among his best creations and rather more successful in fact than the executed restoration.

In his writings, which were as influential in France as the works of Ruskin were in England, he argued that Gothic was the basis for a modern, rational architecture, to be admired for its clarity and economy. The Gothic style was to him the outcome of a lay civilization succeeding the sinister religious domination of the earlier Middle Ages, and he wanted nineteenth-century

methods of construction to compare with the construction of a Gothic building, but using new materials such as iron for supports, framework and rib vaulting. Though renowned for his original ideas, Viollet-le-Duc had less merit as an architect.

GS

LES ABORDS DU CHATEAU

DU CÔTE DE LA DESCENTE A LA BARBACANE

Echelle de 0.01ᵐ pour mètre..

Coupe sur la ligne R.S du plan, feuille n° 14. Restauration. Les hourds sont posés.

Plate 58

CUTHBERT BRODRICK
(1822-1905)

ELEVATION FOR LILLE
CATHEDRAL, FRANCE, 1856
Pen and wash, 12×10in (30.5×25.4cm)
RIBA Drawings Collection, London

In the competition for a new cathedral in Lille, held in 1856, British architects did particularly well. Burges and Clutton came first and George E Street second. Notwithstanding that, a Frenchman, Lassus, who took third place, eventually designed the executed building. Brodrick's essay in French thirteenth-century Gothic is not nearly as assured and knowledgeable as the prizewinners' entries: with its extravagant open arcades and thin spire, it is more typical of the earlier Gothic Revival before it was put on a serious archaeological basis. Possibly Brodrick was trying to please the French judges; possibly he was unhappy with the style, for he was essentially a Classicist and is principally remembered for designing Leeds Town Hall. This freely drawn pen elevation of the west front does, however, have a certain vitality in its use of thirteenth-century detail culled from Wells, Westminster and elsewhere.

GS

Plate 59

GEORGE EDMUND STREET
(1824-81)

INTERIOR PERSPECTIVE FOR THE
NATIONAL GALLERY, LONDON,
1866
Sepia pen, $21\frac{1}{2} \times 17\frac{1}{3}$ in $(55 \times 44$ cm$)$
RIBA Drawings Collection, London

For the competition for rebuilding the National Gallery, in which he was in fact unsuccessful, Street submitted this design for the entrance hall. Street was the greatest and most creative Mid-Victorian Gothic Revivalist, and he, like Pugin, believed that Gothic was suitable for all types of building although he was primarily a church architect. He was a very accomplished draughtsman but an obsessive worker, which meant that he never had time to prepare finished rendered perspectives. Instead, he drew perspectives in ink in a style which combined expressive freedom with great precision of detail and form. The complexities of staircases and levels, which Gothicists enjoyed, are here convincingly conveyed.

Street was eventually successful in the competition held in the same year for the Royal Courts of Justice, his principal secular building.

GS

Plate 60

WILLIAM HENRY PLAYFAIR
(1790-1857)

EARLY PROJECT FOR THE ROYAL
INSTITUTION (NOW THE ROYAL
SCOTTISH ACADEMY), THE
MOUND, EDINBURGH, 1820
Pencil and watercolour, 10½×14¼in
(26.6×36.1cm)
The National Gallery of Scotland,
Edinburgh

Playfair's formative years were spent in the vanguard of the Greek Revival with William Stark, Benjamin Wyatt, Robert Smirke and possibly David Laing.

This somewhat mysterious watercolour entitled 'Sketch of Buildings proposed to be erected on the Mound as seen from the Eastern End of Princes Street', appears to have originally related to the 1820 proposals for a row of public buildings on the Mound, for which Thomas Hamilton had also prepared designs. As first painted it originally showed three colonnaded buildings, those on the left and right being tinted out, presumably when Playfair was instructed in 1821-2 to design a building to house the Royal Society, the Society of Antiquaries and the Board for Manufactures which financed the project. As erected at the northern end of the Mound in 1822-6, it was only one-third the length of that here proposed and somewhat different in design, but was duly enlarged to similar proportions in 1832-5, albeit with distyle end porticoes instead of hexastyle central ones. The general concept of this first scheme was, however, realised thirty years later in his final design for the National Gallery, which stands roughly on the same site and echoes it in composition.

DW

Plate 61

ROBERT WILLIAM BILLINGS
(1813-74)

SIDE ELEVATION FOR CASTLE
WEMYSS, WEMYSS BAY,
RENFREWSHIRE, 1853
Pen and wash, 11¾×15in (30×38cm)
RIBA Drawings Collection, London

Billings was articled to John Britton at the age of thirteen, learned architectural drawing under Frederick Mackenzie, and developed a very personal style of draughtsmanship in which great sharpness and precision of line was enlivened by vivid dashes of wash. Invited to Scotland by William Burn in the mid 1840s to undertake *The Baronial and Ecclesiastical Antiquities of Scotland,* he afterwards established there a select architectural practice which enabled him to express his somewhat unorthodox ideas on architecture. In its practice he emulated the masterbuilders of the Middle Ages, executing his own sculpture, but as a designer he was a Scottish baronial equivalent to Teulon, with a marked predilection for angular forms, plate tracery and trapezoidal and multangular arches.

Billings designed lodges at Gosford, the remodelling of Dalziel Castle and additions at Edinburgh and Stirling Castles, but his largest works were for Glasgow magnates. These included warehouses for Sir James Campbell and Castle Wemyss for Sir George Burns Bt (1795-1890), founder of G & J Burns, shipowners and joint founders of the Cunard Line. A preliminary scheme for the nucleus of the castle is shown here. Burns retired to it in 1860 and with his son John, later Lord Inverclyde, subsequently had it extended southwards into a rambling, stepped, U-plan pile with a pier, from which their steam yacht *Capercailzie RYS* provided their personal maritime needs. Billings was still engaged on the project at his death in November 1874. The castle was demolished some years after the Second World War.

DW

Plate 62

EMMANUEL BRUNE (1836-86)

SECTION OF THE PRINCIPAL STAIRCASE FOR THE PALACE OF A SOVEREIGN, 1863
Watercolour (dimensions unavailable)
École Nationale Supérieure des Beaux Arts, Paris

Brune's solution to this somewhat impractical project won him the *Grand Prix* in 1863. Unlike the majority of competition programmes, this one required students to design only several interrelated parts of a building, not the whole. On the right-hand side of this drawing Brune has shown a *porte-cochère* which leads into a vast vestibule. From the vestibule a stairway rises to the level of two colonnaded galleries, which eventually lead to a reception room and a chapel. On the left of the drawing, behind the columns that form an exedra at the half-landing, Brune has given an indication of a garden. The fountain/grotto shown below the equestrian statue is surrounded by stairways leading from the garden up to the first floor. The arrangement of these spaces is controlled by axial symmetries and hierarchial sizing of rooms.

In its florid Renaissance style the design owes much to Charles Garnier's Opéra drawings, which spectacularly revealed both the grandeur and the spatial complexity of his building. This drawing also reveals the subtle qualification of each of the various spaces with different materials. In general, the more majestic rooms are treated with the more precious and highly polished materials. The ceiling is, of course, the most elaborate surface. It was traditionally the place where deities and heroes were represented, and here Brune has indicated typical figures, but has executed the details in a very stylized, almost technical, manner.

The production of such well-finished drawings of elevations, plans and, above all, sections of public buildings at the École des Beaux Arts did much to encourage a firm grasp of planning, circulation and spatial flow in the students.

GS & DL

Plate 63

SIR MATTHEW DIGBY WYATT
(1820-77)

PERSPECTIVE SECTION FOR
THE NATIONAL GALLERY,
LONDON, 1866
Pen and grey wash, 41×26 in
(104×66 cm)
RIBA Drawings Collection, London

In the abortive competition for rebuilding Wilkins' despised Greek Revival building in Trafalgar Square, London, Matthew Digby Wyatt submitted a design in an eclectic Renaissance style. His drawings were particularly fine and his cutaway perspective a notably impressive achievement. By cutting a section through the building and using perspective, Wyatt shows both the façade and the interior in one drawing. This type of drawing is very informative and very difficult to execute successfully; unlike the axonometric which, in a stylized manner, also conveys three-dimensional form, this drawing does not rely on a standard geometrical convention but requires complex setting-up on perspective principles. By showing an impossible slice through a building, with realistic people walking about regardless, a cutaway perspective is a more rarified concept than a conventional perspective and has an almost surreal quality.

GS

Plate 64

ALFRED WATERHOUSE
(1830-1905)

*PERSPECTIVE OF THE NATURAL
HISTORY MUSEUM, LONDON,
1878*
Pencil, sepia pen and watercolour,
20¾×26½in (52.7×67.3 cm)
RIBA Drawings Collection, London

Alfred Waterhouse is a slightly puzzling figure: he was one of the most ruthlessly pragmatic of Gothic Revivalists who was yet an artist of great sensitivity and skill. The perspectives he prepared of his buildings were sometimes considered to be as good as the work of any professional painter. Waterhouse's Natural History Museum was in the Romanesque style but used coloured terracotta and iron construction, and both of these features, as well as the elaborate ornament, are visible in this drawing, in which Waterhouse has triumphed over the difficulty of drawing elliptical arches in perspective. The view is that of the Central Hall seen from the entrance, and the exact realism of the drawing – prepared before the building was finished – can be appreciated if one stands in the same position in the Museum today.

GS

Plate 65

WILLIAM BURGES (1827-81)

SKETCH FOR A FOUNTAIN FOR
THE CITY OF GLOUCESTER, 1856
Pen and watercolour over pencil,
21×17¼in (53.5×44.5cm)
Victoria and Albert Museum, London

Burges, one of the most eccentric and Romantic of English Gothic Revivalists, affected to despise the sophisticated drawings of his contemporaries and adopted a thick black line in the manner of Villard d' Honnecourt. He even published a book of his own drawings inspired by Villard's celebrated Medieval architectural sketchbook. Burges's Neo-Medievalism is very evident in this drawing, as is a certain extravagant crudeness – Burges was very myopic. When entering competitions he was careful to employ the accomplished Swedish perspectivist and draughtsman, Axel Haig.

GS

Plate 66

*RICHARD NORMAN SHAW
(1831-1912)*

*BIRD'S-EYE VIEW OF LEYSWOOD,
GROOMBRIDGE, SUSSEX, 1868*
*Pen and ink, 22½×33 in
(57.5×84cm)*
RIBA Drawings Collection, London

Norman Shaw changed the direction of English architecture away from the Gothic Revival and towards the new vernacular domestic styles – 'Old English' and 'Queen Anne' – as much by his drawings as by his executed buildings. This Romantic bird's-eye view of his first important 'Old English' house was the sensation of the Architecture Room at the Royal Academy in 1870. Shaw had a firm grasp of perspective technique and a free style in pen which lent itself admirably to the new reproduction method of photolithography. This drawing was published in 1871 and, along with the many other fine drawings Shaw produced in the 1870s, it was immensely influential, not least on the other side of the Atlantic where 'Old English' was translated into the Shingle Style.

GS

1776.

CENTENNIAL EXHIBITION + PHILADELPHIA + MAIN PAVILION + INTERIOR VIEW +

Plate 67

THOMAS WISEDELL (1846-84)

PERSPECTIVE OF THE HALL FOR THE CENTENARY EXIBITION, PHILADELPHIA, PENNSYLVANIA, 1876, BY CALVERT VAUX (1824-95) AND G K RADFORD, 1873
Pen and ink (dimensions unavailable)
John Maas, Philadelphia

Working with the engineer G K Radford, the English-born architect and landscape designer Calvert Vaux won the competition for a structure to contain the American Centenary Exhibition, but their extraordinary and imaginative design was not built. The use of iron and glass for exhibition buildings had been established by the Crystal Palace in London in 1851, but architects wished to develop beyond so largely utilitarian a structure and combine richness of ornament with the grandeur of engineering. This Vaux and Radford certainly achieved. Their design envisaged a series of cathedral-like naves, with huge arches rising from piers which served as shops; they wrote that 'The various parts of the building are included in one grand whole, and the result becomes a spacious hall, adequate to the emergencies of the occasion, with long vistas, central and intermediate points of emphasis, direct lines of transit throughout its length and breadth, diagonal lines of communication where really needed, and an entire relief from any appearance of contradiction anywhere, for the visitor is always in an apartment over 200 feet wide, that opens without any intermediate corridor into other apartments also over 200 feet wide.'

Vaux and Radford's draughtsman served them well, for he succeeds in suggesting the extravagance of the interior space by taking an elevated viewpoint and an angle of vision of almost 90° without any serious distortion. He also made his own job more difficult by taking a viewpoint off the central axis. Thomas Wisedell was an English-born architect who went to the USA in 1868 to work for the firm of Vaux and Withers. In 1879 he entered into partnership with Kimball and designed theatres before his early death.

GS

Plate 68

ARTHUR BERESFORD PITE
(1861-1934)

DESIGN FOR A WEST END
CLUBHOUSE, 1822
Pen and ink, 40½×25 in
(102.5×63.5 cm)
RIBA Drawings Collection, London

Although this drawing won Beresford Pite the RIBA's Soane Medallion in 1882, its extreme and archaic Romanticism was much criticized, and it is hard to believe that Pite was wholly serious in presenting this answer to the problem of designing a gentleman's club. Pite was here paying tribute to the Neo-Medieval drawings of William Burges of two decades earlier, which were themselves influenced by the drawings of Dürer.

Pite, who became a very interesting and very idiosyncratic architect, never shed this grotesque drawing style and always signed his drawings with a monogram similar to Dürer's. The city, drawn in distorted perspective, in which he places this Wagnerian fantasy is not London but a product of Pite's extravagant imagination. This drawing is far removed from the contemporary work of the École des Beaux Arts in France, and is one of the happiest products of British Victorian architectural Romanticism.

GS

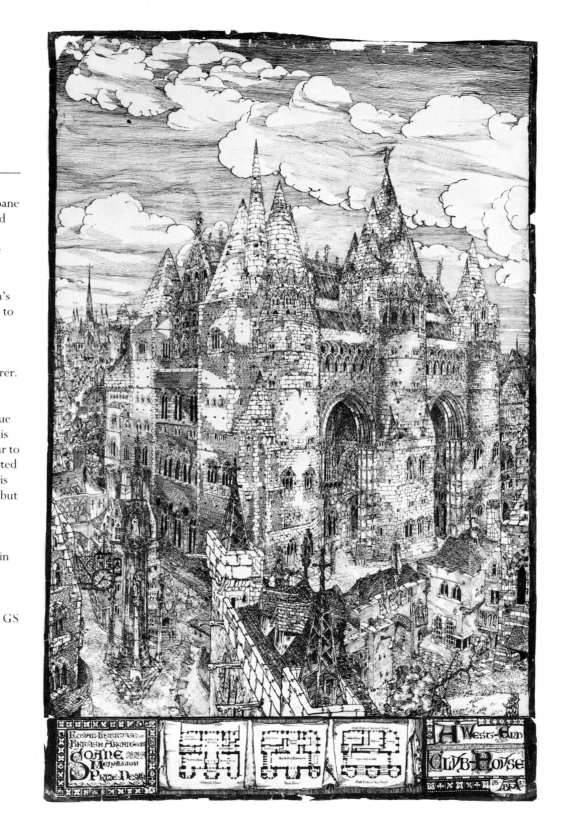

Plate 69

CHARLES GARNIER (1825-98)

*STUDY FOR THE DECORATIONS
FOR THE ARC DE TRIOMPHE,
PARIS, 1885*
*Ink and brush over pencil, 8²/₅ × 12¹/₆ in
(21.2 × 30.9 in)*
Bibliothèque-Musée de l'Opéra, Paris

Garnier, architect of the Paris
Opéra, was in charge of the
public decorations for the funeral of
the writer Victor Hugo, who, when
he died, was regarded as a national
hero and buried in the Panthéon.
Garnier's design was for draping
Chalgrin's Arc de Triomphe, below
which Hugo's catafalque was to be
set. Designing temporary
decorations for public *fêtes* and
funerals was a frequent subject for
students at the École des Beaux Arts
and this bold, free, heavily inked
sketch, or *parti,* is as typical of the
École as the more precise techniques
usually associated with it: in
competitions, the production of a
parti, showing the student's ideas,
preceded the production of finished
geometrical drawings.

GS

Plate 70

HENRY HOBSON RICHARDSON (1838-86)

*PERSPECTIVE STUDY FOR MARSHALL FIELD
WHOLESALE STORE, CHICAGO, c 1885*
*Pencil, black crayon and red wash heightened with white,
on buff paper, 11⅜×9⅞ in (28.9×50.5 cm)*
The Houghton Library, Harvard University, Cambridge

Arguably the greatest of Victorian architects, HH Richardson synthesized the French and English traditions in architecture. His rugged Romanesque designs, which revel in the weight and texture of stone, seem to derive from High Victorian Gothic, from Ruskin and Street, but his clear, logical plans are a consequence of his training at the École des Beaux Arts in Paris during the American Civil War. This expressive free sketch, or *parti,* of the long-destroyed department store of 1885-7 with its tiers of regular round arches, is typical of Richardson's design method; almost every drawing known to be by him is a similarly impressionistic image. Such sketches would be given to his talented assistants, among whom was Stanford White, who would work up the idea into more finished geometrical drawings.

GS

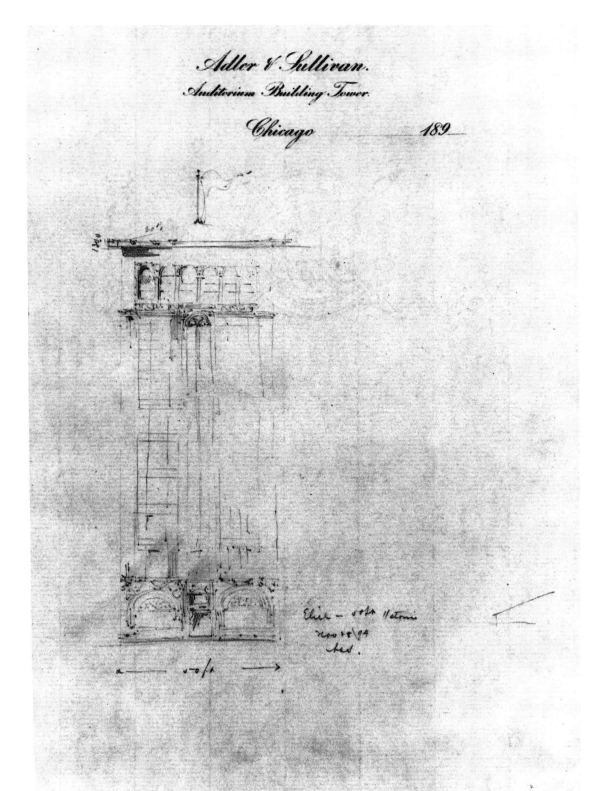

Adler & Sullivan.

Auditorium Building Tower.

Chicago _____ 189__

Plate 71

LOUIS HENRY SULLIVAN (1856-1924)

SKETCH ELEVATION FOR THE ELIEL BUILDING, CHICAGO, 1894
Pen on imprinted Adler & Sullivan stationery,
11½ × 8 in (29.2 × 20.3 cm)
Avery Architectural Library, Colombia University, New York

Although by no means the inventor of the skyscraper, Sullivan was the first American architect to give the tall building coherent artistic form. He recognized that what is important is the base, seen at street level, and the top, which is seen looking up from a distance. The floors in between can be repeated almost indefinitely. This formula can be seen in this sketch design in which the base has large arched openings and the top storey is also arcaded, and surmounted by a boldly projecting cornice and a low-pitched pyramidal roof. The number of storeys is indeterminate and indicated only by the annotation 'Eliel – 50 ft 11 stories/ Nov 28 94/ LS'; and the height: 130 feet. The drawing also reflects Sullivan's other important contribution to architecture: his development of a stylized naturalistic form of 'organic' architectural ornament which seems to anticipate *l'art nouveau.* This decoration was used on the buildings of Adler & Sullivan (his employers) at strategic points; it appears in the entrance motifs of his major building, the Carson, Pirie & Scott Store in Chicago.

Sullivan's scratchy expressive sketches, often using dots, may reflect the year he spent at the École in Paris in the 1870s in between working in Chicago. The sketch is drawn on the office writing paper; the address is that of Adler & Sullivan's greatest building in Chicago, built in 1886-90. This unexecuted project was probably for an apartment building for Dankmar Adler's friend, Levy A Eliel.

GS

THE SCHOOL BOARD OF GLASGOW · MARTYRS PUBLIC SCHOOL

Plate 72

CHARLES RENNIE MACKINTOSH (1868-1928)

PERSPECTIVE OF MARTYRS PUBLIC SCHOOL, GLASGOW, 1896

Pen and ink, 24×36⅜ in (61×92.5 cm)
The Mackintosh Collection, University of Glasgow

The son of a police superintendent, Mackintosh had to overcome parental scepticism before he was able to article himself to a rather uninspired architect, John Hutchison, whose detail he briefly enlivened at Wylie Hill's store in Buchanan Street. In 1889 he secured a place in one of the leading offices, that of the scholarly John Honeyman (1831-1914) and his partner John Keppie (1862-1945), a pupil of Jean Louis Pascal and thus a member of the exclusive Glasgow Beaux Arts clique which included John James Burnet and his partner John A Campbell.

Mackintosh's earliest drawings, both for the firm and for student competitions, were strongly coloured by the Neo-Greek, Beaux Arts and early Renaissance stylistic preferences of the partners, and it is only in the unmistakably fluent penmanship of the figure sculpture, and in the lettering, that there are hints of what was to come. Greater freedom and an acknowledgment of his gifts (in the decision to allow him to design as well as draw out) came in the wake of his Italian study tour of 1891, but his three earliest buildings were still in the Scots Renaissance manner that Keppie had adopted under the influence of his friend Campbell.

Mackintosh made similarly styled pen perspectives of all three buildings. The first was the soaring Glasgow Herald Building (1893-4), the second Queen Margaret College (1895-6), a much smaller turreted building set in a formal garden, and the third, the example illustrated, Martyrs School (1895-6). Although the last built, in style it was externally the least adventurous of the three because so much of the design was dictated by the standard board-school plan. The detailing was still largely Burnet-Keppie Baroque with broad architraves, some banded together, concave-faired balconies and widely spaced balusters, but his emergent individuality is seen in the sinuous curves of the smaller details such as in the wrought-iron lampstandard, and in the composition of the staircase section and the construction of the hall roof within, both of which anticipate features of the Glasgow School of Art, designed the following year.

Mackintosh's brilliant penmanship strongly reflects the influence of Alexander MacGibbon, briefly a colleague in the Honeyman and Keppie office, who worked mainly freelance providing the leading Glasgow offices with much-admired perspectives intended to impress clients and the building journals. MacGibbon, however, could never have drawn such a haunting sky, and the lively journalistic street scenes he favoured are entirely absent. Within a few years the MacGibbon style of draughtsmanship was to be entirely given up for the simple linear treatment with pale watercolour washes which more modern reproduction methods had made acceptable to publishers.

Martyrs School, long threatened by inner ring-road motorway works, has been reprieved and partly repaired, although its future is not yet fully resolved.

DW

HOVSE TO BE BVILT AT GARTMEL FELL GILLHEAD BY WINDERMERE
FOR J·W·BVCKLEY·ESQ^RE   C·F·A·VOYSEY·ARCH^T

GROVND·PLAN

FIRST FLOOR PLAN

Plate 73

CHARLES FRANCIS ANNESLEY
VOYSEY (1857-1941)

PERSPECTIVE AND PLANS FOR
MOORCRAG, WINDERMERE, 1900
Watercolour, 21×16 in (53.5×41 cm)
RIBA Drawings Collection, London

Voysey manages to represent both garden and entrance fronts and the ground and first-floor plans of this house on one sheet of paper. With its sweeping planes of roof and exaggerated chimneys, bands of leaded-light windows and roughcast facing, this is a quintessential Voysey house. Voysey's working drawings, clearly coloured and with distinctive lettering, have a characteristic style, but he was much less accomplished as a perspectivist. His perspectives were often done by other artists, but always they have a rather stiff, naïve quality – like the architecture itself, perhaps – with rather garish colouring. Voysey disliked the clever draughtsmanship of Mackintosh and the Glasgow 'Spook School'.

GS

DE·NIEUWE·BEURS·OP·HET·DAMRAK·TE·AMSTERDAM·GEZIEN·KOMENDE·VAN·DEN·DAM.

Plate 74

HANDRIK PETRUS BERLAGE
(1856-1934)

PERSPECTIVE OF THE NEW
EXCHANGE, AMSTERDAM,
HOLLAND, c 1897-8
Pen and brown ink, 25½×38½ in
(64.8×97.8 cm)
RIBA Drawings Collection, London

Both as an architect and as a draughtsman, H P Berlage was responsible for developing Dutch architecture to the position of eminence and creative originality it enjoyed in the early twentieth century. A product of the Gothic Revival and the writings of Viollet-le-Duc, Berlage's architecture concentrated on the organic expression of structure and showed remarkable creative development during his long career.

This perspective shows his third design for the New Exchange which, with small modifications, was built in 1898-1903. This line drawing does not indicate that the building was to be of brick but it does show the architect's concentration on unbroken wall surfaces which respect the street lines and on the rational disposition of openings and windows. In the background can be seen P J H Cuypers' Central Railway Station. In style, this drawing may be compared with the best European architectural drawings of the 1890s, and the use of integrated artistic lettering was to become a speciality of Dutch architects in the early years of this century. Berlage was awarded the RIBA Gold Medal in 1932, and his family gave this perspective to the Drawings Collection in 1963.

GS

Plate 75

SIR ERNEST GEORGE (1839-1922)

*PERSPECTIVE OF HOUSES IN
HARRINGTON GARDENS, LONDON,
1883*
Pen and sepia ink, 19⁷⁄₈ × 33 in
(50.5 × 83.5 cm)
The Victoria and Albert Museum, London

These houses were designed by George & Peto for individual clients; the one on the far left was built for the librettist W S Gilbert who had lately written *Patience*. Although the houses were built almost simultaneously and have similar plans, each is as different as possible from its neighbour, reflecting a development that was one of the most extreme manifestations of the Victorian fear of uniformity. Ernest George took Norman Shaw's gabled 'Queen Anne' style, combining Renaissance with native associations, and gave it a more German emphasis and also made it more extravagant.

George was a skilled watercolourist, sketcher and etcher, and each year he would return from Continental tours and make good use of the sketches he had made in his eclectic and charming designs. Fortunately he was able to transfer the picturesque variety of his drawings into the executed buildings, which are among the best of Late Victorian English architecture and are beautifully detailed and finished. Ernest George's importance was reflected in the fact that so many of his assistants became famous Arts and Crafts architects who likewise drew their inspiration from the old English traditions, but whose style was simpler. These included Herbert Baker (1862-1946), who reconstructed the interior of the Bank of England between 1930-40, and Edwin Lutyens (see Plate 82). George's etchings and pen drawings have a rather sketchy, sentimental line; as a water colourist he was splendid.

GS

Plate 76

JULES GUÉRIN (1866-1946)

AERIAL PERSPECTIVE OF THE PLAN OF CHICAGO BY DANIEL HUDSON BURNHAM (1846-1912) AND EDWARD H BENNETT (1874-1954), 1909
Watercolour on paper, 29⅜×41¼ in
(74.6×104.8 cm)
Burnham Library of Architecture, The Art Institute of Illinois, Chicago

The full title of this drawing is: 'Chicago, View Looking West, of the Proposed Civic Centre Plaza and Buildings, Showing It as the Center of the System of Arteries of Circulation and of the Surrounding Country', and it portrays the ideals of the American 'City Beautiful' movement: great open spaces and streets receding into infinity, separated by grand Classical buildings.

Burnham had an important influence on the development of the vigorous style of commercial architecture in Chicago, and was largely responsible for the Columbian Exposition in Chicago which took place in 1893, and established the taste for large-scale Classicism in the USA. He later became the country's leading town planner. Ironically, however, Burnham was one of the few important American architects of the period not to have been trained at the École des Beaux Arts, but his renderer, Jules Guérin, had studied painting in Paris. Although informative by adopting an elevated viewpoint, Burnham's perspective is a little pedestrian in taking an axial view of an axial plan; the drama is given by Guérin, who, with rich, purplish colours, shows the city lights reflecting off wet streets at dusk. American-born Guérin was the most inspired perspectivist working for 'American Renaissance' architects; he would fill in the drawing set up by the architect's office with rich colour, showing the scene in dramatic conditions: at dusk or in the setting sun. He was also a painter and executed murals in the Lincoln Memorial in Washington DC.

GS

Plate 77

P JANÁK (1882-1956) and
O GOTFREUND (1889-1927)

PERSPECTIVE SKETCH FOR THE
ŽIŽKA MONUMENT, PRAGUE,
1913
Charcoal (dimensions unavailable)
Courtesy Ivan Margolius

Artistic movements such as Cubism have always exerted a strong influence on the architecture of the day. The Cubists discarded the system of linear perspective, in use since the Renaissance, and attempted to capture another dimension, that of time, in their paintings. Different views of an object, taken from a variety of angles as if the artist was walking around the form, were fused together in one composition.

Janák was a major force in the Cubist movement and published several important articles setting down the aesthetic principles behind Architectural Cubism. He felt that the function of architecture was often overstressed in the design process and that the architect should concentrate on three-dimensional form and its realization in space.

This sketch was part of a competition entry by Janák and the sculptor O Gotfreund for the Žižka Monument in Prague. Of the many drawings submitted by them, this one probably displays their efforts to the best advantage. The result was a massive structure, more sculpture than architecture, with crystal-like forms grouped together in a pile and the figure of Žižka set within the centre of the monument.

CH

Plate 78

ANTONIO SANT'ELIA (1888–1916)

SKETCH PERSPECTIVE OF A
RAILWAY STATION AND AIRPORT,
1913
Black ink and pencil on paper, 11×8¼in
(28×20.9cm)
Civico Museo Storico 'G Garibaldi',
Como, Italy

The short-lived visionary Antonio Sant'Elia was connected with the Italian Futurists and revelled in the architectural forms of the twentieth century – factories, power stations, stations – as well as in the machines – trains, cars and aeroplanes. His many drawings of imaginary buildings of the future have great power, owing both to the expressionism of the architectural forms and to the use of sharp perspective from acute angles. This free sketch was a preliminary study for a finished drawing of a combined station for trains and aeroplanes which, along with other Futuristic structures, was printed in Sant'Elia's 'L'Architettura Futurista' Manifesto, published in *Lacerba* in 1914. Two years later Sant'Elia was to be a victim of the machines and the war that the Futurists had welcomed so wholeheartedly, before he had had a chance to build anything.

GS

Plate 79

SIR JOHN JAMES BURNET
(1857-1938)

PERSPECTIVE SECTION FOR THE
KING EDWARD VII GALLERIES,
BRITISH MUSEUM, LONDON,
c1912
Pen and tracing paper, 34½×23½ in
(88×60 cm)
RIBA Drawings Collection, London

B orn in Glasgow and trained at the École des Beaux Arts in Paris, J J Burnet brought a new sense of Classical monumentality and rational sophistication in design to London when he was invited to extend Smirke's Greek Ionic British Museum in 1904. This admirably clear drawing is a cutaway perspective which shows the grandeur of the staircase, with giant marble columns rising through several floors and a metal lift-cage of decorative design. Unlike Digby Wyatt's earlier cutaway drawing (Plate 63), the construction of the building is here indicated, with steel girders projecting from the section. This drawing, which is damaged, was a study for a watercolour perspective exhibited at the Royal Academy in 1912 and presented to the Academy as Burnet's Diploma Drawing in 1925.

GS

Plate 80

TONY GARNIER (1869-1948)

*PERSPECTIVE OF HOUSING IN AN
INDUSTRIAL CITY, c 1917*
Pen and pencil (dimensions unavailable)
RIBA Drawings Collection, London

Although, after 1905, Tony Garnier designed several remarkable buildings of reinforced concrete construction when he was municipal architect to the city of Lyons in France, his chief importance was as a theoretical town planner of the industrial age. Trained at the École des Beaux Arts, Garnier rejected Beaux Arts ideas of axial symmetry and formal monumentality in urban design. Having won the *Prix de Rome* in 1899, Garnier spent his time designing an imaginary industrial city. These designs were first submitted in 1904 and then further developed and finally published in 1917 as *Une Cité Industrielle*. Garnier proposed a city of 35,000 inhabitants and then planned the industrial area, the public buildings and housing in a rational and informal manner. The published perspective shows part of the 'Quartier d' Habitation', with individual houses of concrete construction and severe cubic form, but arranged in a manner inspired by the English Garden City ideal. As well as rejecting Beaux Arts styles, Garnier departed from highly finished Beaux Arts drawing methods, and his perspectives have a lively and somewhat naïve quality.

GS

Plate 81

*BERTRAM GROSVENOR GOODHUE
(1869-1924)*

*PERSPECTIVE SKETCH OF A HOUSE,
WESTCHESTER COUNTY, NEW YORK, 1915*
Pencil, 21½×37½ in (54.6×95.25 cm)
John R Rivers Collection, Houston, Texas

Bertram Goodhue, the supreme 'Edwardian' of the United States, was a product of the Gothic Revival but, unlike his sometime partner Ralph Adams Cram, who was passionately committed to an archaeological Gothic Revival, his Gothic vision was not a pedantic, anglophilic one but something progressive and creative. Until 1914 he and Cram worked together in a kind of neo-medieval brotherhood, collaborating on many projects including public as well as religious buildings, with Cram designing the plans and Goodhue controlling the working out of the structure and the details. It was a way of simulating the additive process of Gothic building to which successive generations contributed. Goodhue eventually broke with Cram and began to develop a romantic Classical style. His last building, the Nebraska State Capitol, was an imaginative design far away from the Gothic, though it was influenced by Northern European architecture.

Goodhue's links with Europe are also evident in this most accomplished drawing, which was an unexecuted design for a house for Frederick Peterson. Goodhue was celebrated as a draughtsman who 'drew like an angel', and the Romantic character of this picturesque house on its dramatic, towering site is enhanced by the adoption of the low viewpoint. The scheme is reminiscent of his exact contemporary Lutyens, and the drawing recalls Norman Shaw (see Plate 66), but the draughtsmanship is Goodhue's own speciality, and his drawings are considered to be even more superb than his buildings.

GS

Plate 82

SIR EDWIN LANDSEER LUTYENS
(1869-1944)

DESIGN FOR A MEMORIAL TO THE
MISSING OF THE SOMME,
THIEPVAL, FRANCE, c.1927
*Pen and ink and red crayon, 10×8 in
(25.4×20.5 cm)
RIBA Drawings Collection, London*

Lutyens, the finest Establishment
architect of his day, never drew
perspectives, nor was he an
accomplished draughtsman in the
formal sense. Nevertheless, his
'worm's-eye view' sketches, rapidly
executed, immediately convey the
three-dimensional form of his
designs, and much of his
architectural thinking was done in
terms of such sketches. This one,
drawn on his office writing paper, is
of an early scheme for his Memorial
to the Missing of the Somme, in
which Lutyens's increasingly abstract
Classicism was used for a most
complex and Sublime arched
structure, on which are carved
73,000 names. This sketch indicates
the massing of the memorial and the
hierarchy of arched tunnels
penetrating it along two axes, with
the keystone of one arch at the level
of the springing of the next.

GS

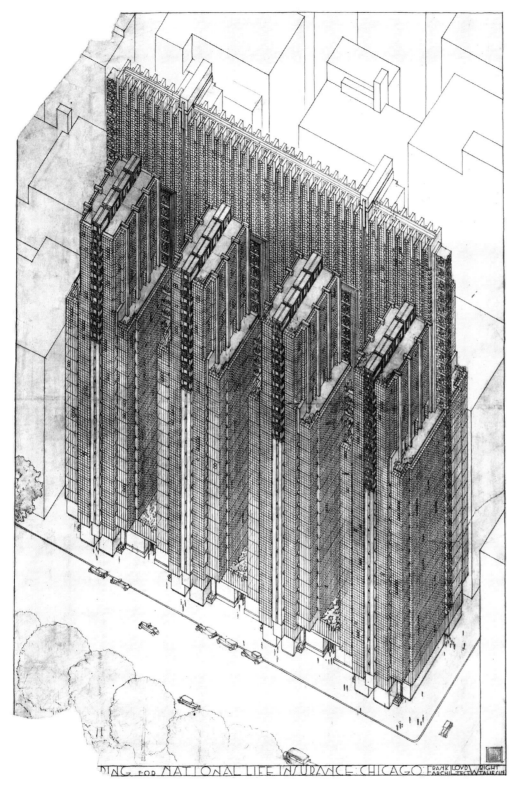

DING FOR NATIONAL LIFE INSURANCE CHICAGO FRANK LLOYD WRIGHT ARCHITECT TALIESIN

Plate 83

FRANK LLOYD WRIGHT
(1867-1959)

AXONOMETRIC PROJECTION OF
THE NATIONAL LIFE INSURANCE
BUILDING, CHICAGO, ILLINOIS,
1924
Pen and ink and coloured pencils on
tracing paper, 45⅝×30¼in
(115.8×76.8cm)
The Frank Lloyd Wright Foundation,
Taliesin, Arizona

A stylish draughtsman who also employed other fine draughtsmen like Marion Mahoney, Frank Lloyd Wright seldom used the axonometric. Instead, his houses were usually drawn in perspective with an economical line and a subtle colouring which owed much to Japanese art. The lettering on this drawing is typical of Wright, however. Wright may have adopted the axonometric, with its mathematical regularity and mechanistic strangeness of impression, as suitable for a skyscraper – this unexecuted design was one of several projects he had designed for A M Johnson since 1920. The complex shape of the building may have been a response to zoning laws, but Wright clearly wished to depart from a simple tower form. Floors are cantilevered out from reinforced concrete piers, and the external finish was to be of glass in copper frames. Lateral wings coming off a central spine allowed light to reach most parts of the building. Although cars and people are introduced, this precise, almost clinical drawing presents a very different view of the City of the Future from the Romantic visions of Hugh Ferriss (see Plates 84 and 85).

GS

Plate 84

HUGH FERRISS (1889-1962)

*PERSPECTIVE OF APARTMENTS ON
BRIDGES, NEW YORK, DESIGNED
BY RAYMOND HOOD (1881-1934),
1929*
Pencil (dimensions unavailable)
Courtesy Alison Sky

The dramatic burgeoning of the skyscraper in the 1920s and the pressure on land in Manhatten generated several bizarre architectural schemes. One of these was proposed by Raymond Hood, who had won the Chicago Tribune Tower Competition of 1922 and who was to design the Daily News and the McGraw-Hill Buildings in New York. Hood imagined great suspension bridges across New York's rivers, with the towers as skyscrapers and with additional apartments suspended from the cables. Landing stages were to be placed at the foot of the towers so that residents could alight from their launch, yacht or hydroplane and be whizzed by a lift to their apartment.

Hood's Chicago Tribune building was a Gothic skyscraper, even though he had been trained at the École des Beaux Arts in Paris. He did not enter the school at his first attempt, however, as he failed in drawing. For this scheme he turned to Hugh Ferriss (see also Plate 85) to give it reality and the artist, in his characteristic style, emphasized the bulk of the form and concentrated on dramatic light and shadow. Ferriss published the scheme in his book *Metropolis of Tomorrow*, published in the same year.

GS

Plate 85

HUGH FERRISS (1889-1962)

PERSPECTIVE OF A SKYSCRAPER,
1922
Charcoal, pencil and crayon,
26¼×20 in (66.5×50.8 cm)
Cooper Hewitt Museum of Decorative
Arts & Design, New York

Hugh Ferriss was the greatest American architectural draughtsman of the twentieth century, who celebrated the Sublime Romance of the skyscraper. As well as executing perspectives of actual proposed buildings, Ferriss also presented a vision of the City of the Future, a city of tall buildings, elevated pavements, lofty terraces, cars and aeroplanes, which he conveyed in his dramatically shaded and lit perspectives, drawn from imaginary aerial positions or looking sharply up, and carried out in a *bravura* style in charcoal and crayon.

Ferriss's fantasies were a development of the form of early twentieth-century New York skyscrapers, and envisaged an architecture of mass, of towering, stepped-back forms and accentuated verticals – very different from the glass-box the skyscraper became.

This drawing was the last of a series of four, prepared for the architect Harvey Wiley Corbett, designed to show the effect of the New York Zoning Law of 1916 on a block 200 by 600 feet, and how the resulting receding mass could be made into a coherent architectural form with carefully modelled set-backs and dramatic power. Analogous to the metropolitan futuristic visions of Sant'Elia or the German Expressionists, and revelling in the pure poetry of architecture, Ferriss's work had a practical application as well.

GS

Plate 86

LE CORBUSIER (1887-1966)

'THE LAW OF THE LAND', 1946
Pen and ink, 5½×8½ in (14×21 cm)
From Le Corbusier, Propos
d'Urbanisme *(Paris, 1946); English
translation by C Entwistle,* Concerning
Town Planning *(London, 1947)*

Le Corbusier was not only a brilliant architect, painter, sculptor and designer but also a prolific author. His books outlined his theories on modern architecture. This one, entitled *Propos d'Urbanisme,* contains his ideas on the proposed reconstruction of Europe after its devastation in World War II. It posed questions such as: 'should we rebuild towns which have been entirely destroyed on old sites, or seek better locations?'; 'where should industrial centres be situated in the towns of the future?'; 'should prefabricated housing be used by architects?'. In the answers provided he set down some of the most rational, far-sighted solutions to the problems of post-war Europe.

Throughout his career he was involved in schemes for cities such as Paris and Algiers. Unfortunately, many of his ideas were rejected as 'impractical'. This sketch of Algiers is an improved version of some of his earlier ideas. He described this plan as a 'magnificent architectural symphony'. In it, he separated the industrial centre from the residential zone, made provisions for a civic centre and buildings which would, in the future, be used to promote interracial harmony between the Arabs and the French. He also rerouted the motorway to take advantage of the magnificent site and establish rapid contact between the different zones.

CH

Plate 87

LE CORBUSIER (1887-1966)

'NATURE IS ENTERED IN THE
LEASE', 1946
Pen and ink, 8½×5½ in (21×14 cm)
From Le Corbusier, Propos
d'Urbanisme (Paris, 1946); English
translation by C Entwistle, Concerning
Town Planning (London, 1947)

This drawing, which appeared in *Concerning Town Planning* in the section on the Town of the Future, demonstrates Le Corbusier's concern with concepts such as the classification of different functions within a city, the city's scale in relation to people and the necessity of housing large densities of population. He felt that houses should no longer follow the roadways; instead, they should 'leave the streets' and form residential 'islands'. To liberate the maximum amount of open land, dwellings should be concentrated in one building, and this building should be raised on stilts. He tells us: 'By this means, the site will be effectively enlarged and made one with the surrounding countryside; seen through the glass wall of the dwelling, the trees and hills and fields become a permanent extension of the home: Nature is entered in the lease.'

Critical opinion on his town-planning schemes is not favourable: 'For all his visionary capacity he never fully appreciated the effect of excesses in transportation and centralization on people'. Could these problems have been foreseen in the immediate post-war period? Dwellers in the cities of today are not even aware that much of what is found there – with its many faults – is the result of his visionary thinking.

CH

HOLZWORTH RESIDENCE GEORGE FRED KECK ARCHITECT

Plate 88

GEORGE FRED KECK (1895-1980)

HOLZWORTH HOUSE, WILMETTE, ILLINOIS, 1930
Watercolour, 11⅝×9⅝ in (28.75×24cm)
The State Historical Society of Wisconsin, Madison, Wisconsin

George F Keck was one of the pioneer architects of the Modern movement in Chicago. In recent years, architectural historians have begun to reassess his contribution to architecture – he is usually overshadowed by Mies van der Rohe, another important architect from Chicago. Keck's work has been described as a mixture of the Beaux Arts and Modern. One of his creations, entitled the House of Tomorrow, was prepared for the Chicago 'Century of Progress' Exposition of 1933-4. It featured a dodecagonal glass house with a hangar for a small aeroplane at its side. Although this seems slightly humorous today, it reflected an early twentieth-century vision of future American travel habits. Keck felt that architecture's primary function should be to answer the needs of the age in which it was created.

This drawing of the Holzworth residence in Illinois was probably used at a presentation to the client or for an exhibition: note the careful lettering at the bottom of the page. A perspective view of the main entrance to the house, it shows a mother and young child standing on the front pathway. According to one critic, 'Keck is making a clear statement about the appropriateness of the modern style to domestic daily life, an issue of understandable concern to an architect intent on building in a non-traditional mode in the American Midwest of the 1930s'.

CH

Plate 89

WILLIAM WALCOT (1874-1943)

SKETCH OF THE MUNICIPAL ART GALLERY, DUBLIN, IRELAND, FOR SIR EDWIN LUTYENS, 1913
Pen and ink and grey wash,
10⅘ × 14⅕ in (27.5 × 36 cm)
RIBA Drawings Collection, London

This unexecuted scheme by Lutyens for a gallery 'bridge' across the River Liffey was promoted by Sir Hugh Lane, most of whose collection of paintings was on loan to the Municipal Art Gallery. Lutyens's design was shown in several perspective watercolours, for which this is a pen sketch prepared by his favourite draughtsman, William Walcot, who was one of the very greatest English architectural draughtsmen.

Walcot, half-Russian, had practised as an architect in Moscow before coming to England as a painter, etcher and architectural draughtsman. He had a particular ability to convey the monumentality of Classical architecture, and he executed a series of etchings of restorations of Roman buildings in all their imaginary original glory. Walcot's perspectives had a free colouring over the outline of the building and were peopled by characteristic shadowy figures.

GS

Plate 90

ELIEL SAARINEN (1873-1950)

*AERIAL PERSPECTIVE OF
CRANBROOK SCHOOL FOR BOYS,
BLOOMFIELD HILLS, MICHIGAN,
1926*
Soft pencil, 25¾×29½ in (65.4×75 cm)
*Cranbrook Academy of Art Museum,
Michigan*

The use of soft pencil for perspective drawings enjoyed a vogue during the early decades of the twentieth century, and Eliel Saarinen was a master of the technique. His bird's-eye view of Cranbrook School indicates the picturesque disposition of the buildings and a range of textures – of building materials and plants – as well as light and shade, yet this great variation in tone is achieved by consistent diagonal shading.

Cranbrook School for Boys was Eliel Saarinen's first commission after he arrived from Finland in the United States in 1923, and it is his best-known building in America. The design was made in 1925 and the buildings erected in 1926-30, with small variations from the aerial perspective. The plan (shown on page 59) was a response to the farm buildings and yards formerly on the site, while the sophisticated Tudor style, with expressionist brickwork and much sculpture, reflected the Arts and Crafts ideals of the client, George G Booth. The form of the tower, however, is strongly reminiscent of Saarinen's masterpiece, Helsinki Railway Station, which was built in 1905-14 before he emigrated to the United States.

GS

Plate 91

RUDOLF SCHINDLER (1887-1953)

*PERSPECTIVE OF A BEACH
HOUSE, CALIFORNIA, 1937*
Coloured crayon, $13\frac{3}{4} \times 12\frac{1}{4}$ in
$(35 \times 31$ cm$)$
Art Galleries of the University of
California, Santa Barbara

Schindler was born and trained
in Vienna but most of his career
was spent in California, where was to
be built this unexecuted project for a
beach house for Rupert R Ryan.
Schindler had trained under Otta
Wagner and had been much
influenced by Loos and Mackintosh.
Even after he emigrated to the USA
he remained in contact with
developments in Europe, and this
typical design, of rectilinear form
with cantilevered balconies, shows
the influence of Rietveld and Dutch
'De Stijl'. This perspective, however,
may well reflect the time Schindler
spent working for Frank Lloyd
Wright. Drawings in coloured
crayon were popular in the 1920s and
1930s, and this bold and clear
perspective emphasizes the complex
cubic form of the building by taking a
low viewpoint, which also reveals its
relationship to the Romantic site.

GS

Plate 92

ALVAR AALTO (1898-1976)

*SKETCH OF 'SHIPS ON THE NILE
BETWEEN LUXOR AND ISNA',
1954-55*
Soft pencil (dimensions unavailable)
The Alvar Aalto Foundation

Alvar Aalto's work has always
stood out in relation to his
contemporaries', who were building
in the International Style. He enjoyed
using rough textures, natural
colours, and adding certain lyrical
touches which were not usually part
of their artistic vocabulary. His
working method was also quite
unusual, and this perhaps explains
the highly individual character of his
structures. He claimed that each
architectural project had a problem,
or series of problems, that seemed
insurmountable. He tried to clear his
mind of all distractions, and began to
draw, simple, almost abstract
drawings, much like this one of
'Ships on the Nile'. The solution to
the problem soon presented itself:
'. . . via this route I eventually arrive
at an abstract basis to the main
concept, a kind of universal
substance with whose help the
numerous quarrelling sub-problems
can be brought into harmony.'

During his trip to Egypt in 1954-5,
Aalto drew the boats on the Nile
many times; he was apparently
fascinated by the often-abstract
configurations they formed when
moving about together on the river.
The travel sketches helped him to
refine his visual sense. This drawing
illustrates his fascination with the
fan-motif, a type of 'universal' form
that was employed in many of his
projects. It appeared in his design for
a chair, in the suspension structure
for a sports centre, and in several
ceiling constructions.

CH

Plate 93

LOUIS I KAHN (1901-74)

SKETCH OF FRANKISH WALLS AT THE ACROPOLIS, ATHENS, GREECE, 1951
Crayon on paper, 11 × 13½ in (27.5 × 33.75 cm)
Richard Oliver, New York

Louis Kahn was one of the most important architects to emerge in America during the post-war period. He stood out from his contemporaries because of his refusal to build exclusively in steel and glass; instead, he championed the use of brick and concrete, and strove to emphasize the building's materials and construction process. Different types of lines used in his drawings often influenced the design project he was working on. His sketches were extremely important to him at each stage of the project because they helped to clarify a particular aesthetic concept. As he put it: 'If we were to train ourselves to draw as we build, from the bottom up, when we do, stopping our pencil to make a mark at the joints of pouring or erecting, ornament would grow out of our love for the expressive method'.

In 1951 he spent a year abroad as the architect-in-residence at the American Academy in Rome. This experience was to have considerable influence on his formal vocabulary. This drawing of the Acropolis at Athens is typical of his travel sketches. He drew highly interpretative views of the different Classical sites; they were brightly coloured with the various architectural elements depicted in strong contrasting tones. In this one he was clearly fascinated by the way in which the walls echo the natural landscape.

CH

Plate 94

PAUL HOGARTH (b.1917)

*PERSPECTIVE OF THE FISK
RUBBER PLANT, CHICOPEE FALLS,
MASSACHUSETTS, 1963*
Pen and ink, 20×15 in (50.8×38.1 cm)
Paul Hogarth, Majorca

Although Hogarth is not a practising architect, he finds architecture extremely stimulating for its reflection of the culture which produced it. He has written many books on the art of drawing, one of the most remarkable of which is *Drawing Architecture* (London, 1974). He states that architecture is 'the embodiment of a daydream about a palace or pub occupied by the memories of people and events long since gone . . .' His drawings express these reactions to the structures of both past and present, and this sketch of the Fisk Rubber Plant in America demonstrates his highly individual style.

As Hogarth points out, artists throughout the ages have reacted differently to the architectural creations in their environment, especially industrial architecture and engineering projects. In the eighteenth and early nineteenth centuries artists viewed such creations with a favourable eye; they believed in progress and the great benefits to be derived for society from mass industrialization. A counter-reaction set in during the mid-nineteenth century, when people began to have mixed reactions about the Industrial Age, with its many social problems. Today, artists such as Hogarth often make challenging statements about modern society and its architecture through their drawings.

CH

Plate 95

SUPERSTUDIO, FLORENCE, 1960s

AERIAL PERSPECTIVE OF NEW YORK EXTRUSION, 1969
Collage and pencil, 36×28 in (91.4×71.12 cm)
The Gilman Paper Company Collection, New York

During the 1960s different groups of avant-garde 'visionary' architects flourished throughout the world, including Archigram in London, the Metabolists in Japan, and the design units Archizoom and Superstudio in Italy. This last group was founded by five architects from Florence University, who sought to redefine the role of the architect in society. They stressed political activism, group projects and an interest in technology, in projects that were often of fantastic proportions, insisting that 'the image is communication'. Much of their work exists as written statements about architecture, and they have also made films which explain their ideas.

In this paper project entitled 'New York Extrusion', from their 'Continuous Monument' series, they have certainly created a powerful and challenging image. The series is subtitled 'An Architectural Model for Total Urbanization', and in it pristine geometrical forms are stretched across the world, housing its entire population. According to Superstudio, monuments stand as reminders of the human search for order. Structures such as Stonehenge or the Pyramids were only the beginning of the total urbanization of the future. In the drawing shown the forms of the future are spread across Manhattan, enveloping the skyscrapers of the past.

CH

BRANT·JOHNSON HOUSE   1975~   VAIL VILLAGE·COLORADO

Plate 96

ROBERT VENTURI (b.1925)

*PERSPECTIVE OF THE BRANT-
JOHNSON HOUSE, VAIL,
COLORADO, 1975*
Pen and ink and applied colour,
21½×28 in (54.6×71.1 cm)
RIBA Drawings Collection, London

Robert Venturi has been widely influential in his attempt to develop beyond the limited disciplines of international modern architecture and to reintroduce the richness and complexity given by historical references. He was possibly the leader of the trend towards reviving the symbolism in buildings with the use of historic detail such as pitched roofs, an emphasis on doors and windows as 'features' and an increased use of colour. From the early 1960s onwards the standard rectangular shape of modern buildings has been broken down gradually into more interesting forms, particularly in private houses, where there are the greatest opportunities for individualists to produce interesting buildings in a vernacular style, using traditional forms to produce a homely feeling. In this perspective of a holiday house, Venturi emphasizes its homely domestic character by adopting a stylized naïve drawing manner reminiscent of European pen and ink drawings of around 1900.

GS

Plate 97

LEON KRIER (b. 1925)

*PERSPECTIVE OF SOCIAL CENTRE,
PIAZZA S. PETRO, ROME, ITALY,
1977*
*Pen and ink 11¾×16½ in
(29.8×41.9 cm)*
Property of the artist, London

The Luxembourg-born architect Leon Krier has been an influential force in architecture in the last decade, through his drawings of ideal projects not intended to be executed. This drawing is part of his *Roma Interrotta* project, in which Krier, along with eleven other architects, was invited to take part in a theoretical exercise in town planning based on portions of Giambattista Nolli's eighteenth-century plan of Rome. Krier has been anxious to re-establish the importance of public spaces and public buildings in European cities and has a great understanding of the historical relationship between urban monumentality and complexity, in contrast to the destructive utopian town planning of the twentieth century. Between the giant piers of this strange structure, over a space which is both enclosed and open, can be seen the dome of St Peter's and Bernini's colonnade.

Many of Krier's designs are monumental and Neo-Classical in style, and his drawings revive the linear perspective technique of Schinkel, and these interests had a profound influence on the designs and drawing manner of James Stirling when Krier worked for him. In this case, by adopting an elevated viewpoint to give the typical Schinkel-esque diagonal view, the perspective rather minimizes the colossal scale of the building.

GS

THW
South Elevation

Plate 98

QUINLAN TERRY (b. 1937)

PART ELEVATION OF BAHAI TEMPLE, 1976,
DESIGNED BY RAYMOND ERITH (1904-73)
AND QUINLAN TERRY
Pen and ink, 53×30 in (134.6×76.2 cm)
Raymond Erith and Quinlan Terry

For many years one of the few redeeming features in the Architecture Room at the Royal Academy were the beautifully finished elevations of designs by Raymond Erith. Later these were sometimes drawn by Erith's assistant, partner and successor Quinlan Terry, who now occupies a unique position in England by maintaining the Palladian Classical tradition. This drawing is typical of the firm's precision and style, although the exotic nature of this unexecuted project is less usual. This is part of the south elevation of a circular domed temple and is minutely finished and carefully shaded with tiny ink dots in a manner worthy of the old Beaux Arts tradition.

GS

Plate 99

JAMES WINES (b. 1932) FOR SITE INC.,
ARCHITECTS

PERSPECTIVE OF FOREST BUILDING, 1978
Pen and ink on white paper, 14×17 in (35×42.5 cm)
James Wines and Alison Sky, Site, New York

In the words of James Wines, 'Site Inc. is a multi-disciplinary architecture and environmental arts group chartered for the purpose of exploring new concepts for the urban visual environment . . . This work . . . is often suspended between the definitions of art and architecture – and is usually characterized by social, political, and architectural commentary.' This drawing for Best Products Inc. is typical of his work. The site was surrounded by a dense forest and one of the requirements was that a maximum number of trees must be preserved. Wines allowed the trees to envelop and even penetrate the Best Showroom, as seen in this fine sketch.

CH

RICHMOND BEST SHOWROOM

Wines
SITE 1978

Plate 100

ERIC PARRY (b.1952)

SECTION THROUGH A POLITICAL BUILDING, 1982
Coloured pencil on white paper, 114 in sq (290 cm sq)
Property of the artist

This political building was conceived as an informal place for meetings and political conversations, and designed to be situated between an existing railway and a proposed new square in North London. The drawing shown here illustrates a sequence of spaces as they would reveal themselves to a person moving through the building. Starting at the foyer on the second level above the square and bypassing the internal atrium, one can either enter a large dome-covered lecture hall or descend into a theatre and political cabaret connected with the garden. Ascending the staircase one arrives at club rooms, a large hall and a school of rhetoric. In the background one can see the silhouette of the hotel for visitors.

This drawing is an eloquent illustration of the power of different materials, light and spatial transparencies, that is, their contribution to the creation of the appropriate identity and meaning of particular spaces. The tension between the hidden parts of the building and the fully visible parts is not only a characteristic of the drawing but also the very essence of the space as it was understood in this project.

DV

Plate 101

NIGEL WESTBROOK (b. 1954)

*SECTIONAL ELEVATION THROUGH
THE CLOISTER OF A MONASTERY,
1982*
*Coloured pencil on tracing paper,
236×177 in (600×450 cm)*
Property of the artist

The image of a new monastic
building situated in the centre of
a contemporary town is as unusual
today as it was normal in a town of
the medieval period. The building of
a Dominican monastery, illustrated
here, refers to a long tradition of
religious urban orders whose role
was to live not only their own
spiritual life but, more importantly,
to contribute to the everyday life of
the town. The way in which this
building embodies both these roles is
expressed in this section through the
cloister, where the main building
round the cloister is treated as a
house but its domesticity is
challenged by explicitly non-
domestic elements such as towers,
arcades and portals. Most of the
rooms face both the inside and the
outside world. In the cloister, which
is the intimate and symbolically most
important part of the monastery, the
building loses its neutrality and to
some extent its monumentality, and
becomes part of the interior,
designed with such primary elements
as stone, earth and vegetation.
Seen as a whole, the monastery is a
careful balance of many
contradictory requirements, such as
the sacred and profane,
monumentality and domesticity,
exteriority and interiority, and
urbanity and rusticity.

DV

Plate 102

FRANCO RAGGI (b.1945)

UNSTABLE ELEMENT IN THE
DESERT: THE COLUMN, 1976
Pen and ink sketch, 8¼×11½in
(21×29cm)
Property of the artist, Milan

Like the drawing by Wines (Plate 99), this sketch challenges our traditional approaches to architecture. A column stands alone in the midst of the desert, seemingly held aloft by four guy ropes. According to Raggi, architecture is inherent in objects 'since they are the media of primary actions with a sense of "generality" which is the typical character of architecture (of the archetype)'. Here he chooses one of architecture's archetypes, the column, to make a statement about the ever-changing relationships of objects. The column, traditionally the load-bearing element, is held in position by the guy ropes which, in turn, are usually used to support flimsy structures such as canvas awnings and tents.

CH

APPENDIX

GLOSSARY

It has been stated that architectural drawings can be divided into two distinct types, the construction drawing and the presentation drawing. While it is true to say that their primary function is generally the same, that is, to provide sufficient information to construct a building, it is also true that in recent times there has been a divergence between the two types. The presentation drawing has tended to become less frequent, more seductive and thus more publicized. Construction drawings, being of necessity more factual, have correspondingly decreased in popularity for various reasons, not the least of which is the misconception that they are only produced for the builder. It is therefore possible for the interested non-expert to miss the opportunity of viewing some of the most interesting works of architects past and present, for no other reason than his or her inability to understand the basic forms of construction drawing. Much of the enjoyment of studying an attractive subject stems from an understanding of all its functions. It is hoped to extend the reader's interest by this short explanation of the more technical forms of architectural drawing.

It is important, first, to appreciate that all drawings are proportionate to the finished structure. This relationship is indicated by a scale which may be shown as a representative fraction ($\frac{1}{96}$), a proportion (1:96), written (one inch = eight feet) or drawn as a subdivided horizontal line. It is not necessary to be able to use these scales, but because drawings are not all produced to the same scale the conventions used will differ in size and complexity. The smaller the figures representing the scale, the larger is the scale; the larger the scale, the bigger and more detailed will be the drawing. When the eye can recognize the same convention on a small-scale drawing *and* a large-scale drawing, then the understanding is nearly complete.

Primary Drawings

As the main purpose of the construction drawing is to impart information, the choice of projection should facilitate this function. The primary drawings – plans, sections and elevations – are orthographic in nature, which is to say that the observer's line of sight is perpendicular to the principal surfaces. Orthographic projection is therefore two-dimensional and has the further advantage that all faces of an object parallel to the drawing surface are represented without distortion or foreshortening. True angles and measurements may therefore be taken off at will. It is in this two-dimensional 'flat' projection that most primary drawings are presented.

GROUND-FLOOR PLAN This is generally the level at which the building is entered. It is actually a sectional bird's-eye view after a horizontal plane has been cut about mid-way between floor and ceiling and the upper part lifted off. The building layout is thus revealed, showing the positions and thickness of external and internal walls (in the example they are line-hatched). Openings in these walls for doors can be recognized by the quarter-circles indicating how they open, and for windows by the light lines representing glazing. It is customary to differentiate between elements which are cut by the horizontal plane and those which are not. Thus the cut surfaces, walls and columns, are given a bold profile while stairs, column bases, window-sills, etc. are shown with a lighter line.

FIRST-FLOOR PLAN The view of this and any subsequent higher level is essentially that of the ground floor, inasmuch as it represents a horizontal mid-way cut with the upper part lifted off. The elements are illustrated in the same style and with the same emphasis. It is, however, not necessarily the same size as the floor below, and to establish the correct relationship the vertical circulation – staircase, lift, ramp or escalator – should be compared, since it will occur in the same position on each floor. The vertical circulation is perhaps the most difficult element to identify because at no one level is a staircase or similar inclined access to another level shown in its entirety. The bottom of the flight is shown on the lower level up to the horizontal cut and then 'disappears'. The rest of the flight appears on the higher-level plan (see the example).

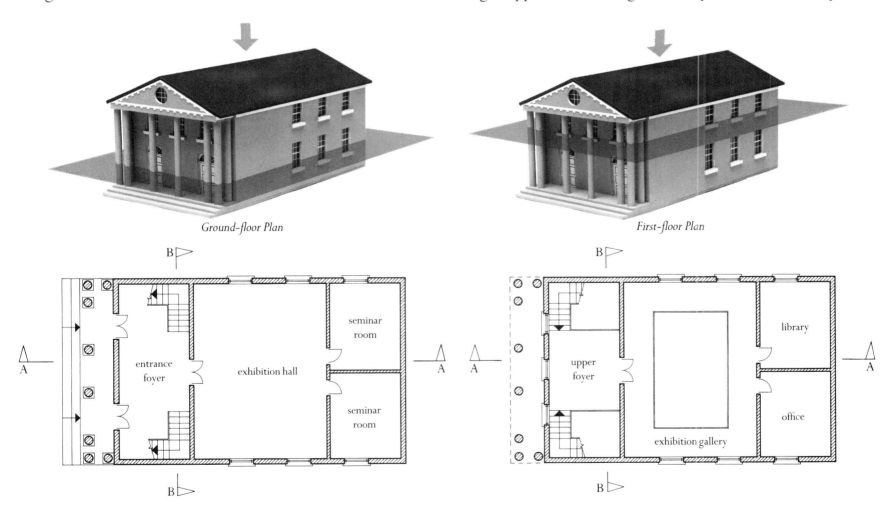

Ground-floor Plan

First-floor Plan

CROSS-SECTION Just as a plan is obtained by the use of a horizontal cutting plane, a cross-section is obtained by making a vertical cut through the shorter axis and, rather like opening a doll's house, taking away that part in front of the cut. The view seen illustrates the main function of the section, i.e. to show the relationship between the horizontal layers – ground, floors, ceilings and roof. The section also forms an important link between plan and elevation, providing the third dimension, height. The same conventions are used to emphasize the cut surfaces, the lighter lines showing elements seen in elevation. It will be noted that the section does not give a view through the whole building but only as far as the next internal wall parallel with the cut.

LONGITUDINAL SECTION The view is obtained in the same way as a cross-section, with a vertical cut, but through a longer axis. The view is restricted, as with all sections, so that the position chosen for the cut has to be carefully considered to make use of another function of the section, which is to obtain the largest number of relationships between interior spaces so that the constructor may readily see how the parts of the building are intended to fit together. These positions are usually indicated on the plans of each level by means of arrows, triangles, bold lines, etc. which point in the direction that the section is to be viewed. As with other sections, the cut material is shown by means of cross hatching with the lines at a 45° angle.

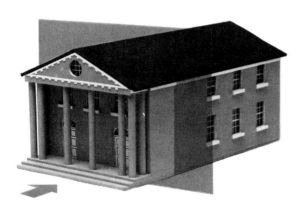

Cross-section B – B

Londitudinal Section A – A

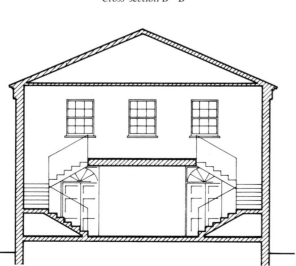

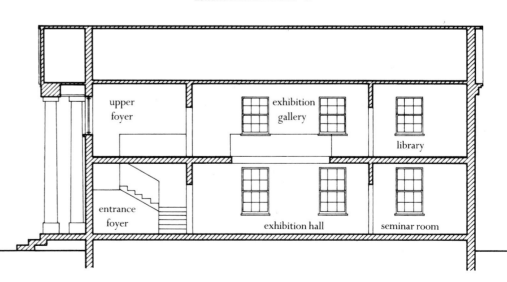

FRONT ELEVATION A front elevation is probably the easiest orthographic drawing to understand because it is a familiar view. There are no cuts as it is a purely external picture and all the elements involved – such as doors, windows, steps and columns – are shown in a projection which is very nearly that which can be seen in any thoroughfare. Elevations convey the building's form and massing, and the front elevation in particular provides the first indication of the building's character.

SIDE ELEVATION As with the front elevation, this is an exterior view of the building but on the axis at right angles to the front elevation. Its function and value is the same in conveying form and massing. In reality the only major dif-ference between construction and presentation elevations is in the latter's use of shade and shadow to convey to an orthographic view the third dimension, that of depth. The relationship between elevations and sections can be readily understood if it is recognized that when the part of the building removed to reveal the section is replaced, the result is an external face, i.e. an elevation.

Pictorial Projections

While orthographic drawings can depict the building in reality, they do so in a fragmented series of related views which, though informative in themselves, do not individually

Front Elevation

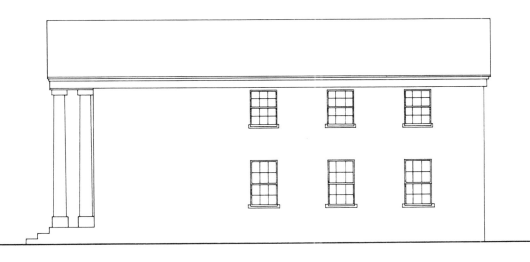

Side Elevation

convey form. Pictorial projections, however, illustrate the three dimensions of form simultaneously, showing the building in a more realistic style. They are easily produced, and provide effective views of the building. With the added advantage of being able to measure off length, breadth and height, they form an important part of the design process. Pictorial projections can be classified into two groups: parallel and perspective. The parallel forms which follow are the most commonly used and illustrate the governing principles.

OBLIQUE These projections will have one face of the object parallel to the plane of projection. There are two main variations: cabinet and planometric.

    CABINET The front face or elevation is drawn as an orthographic elevation, but the receding lines are drawn at half the scale of the front face. If the receding lines were drawn to the same scale, the projection (called in this case Cavalier) would appear distorted and unrealistic to the eye. Using half-scale gives a more natural appearance. The angle of the receding lines can be varied according to the view sought, but $45°$ is commonly used.

PLANOMETRIC With this projection it is the plan form which is drawn to true shape and scale. The third dimension, height, is obtained by the use of vertical projectors drawn to the same scale as the plan. (This is the projection commonly but inaccurately called axonometric. Axonometric is a generic term describing a separate family of projections.) The angle at which the plan form is tilted to provide the three-dimensional view can be varied, but $45°$ or $30°$ is usual.

Oblique (Cabinet) Projection

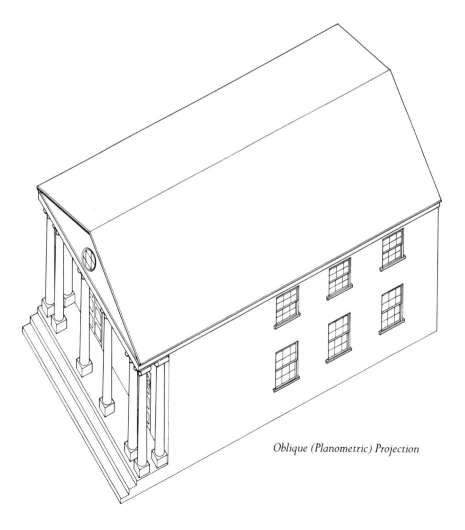

Oblique (Planometric) Projection

ISOMETRIC This projection comes within the generic term axonometric and is probably the best-known and used parallel form. It is similar to planometric in that the basis is the plan, from which the vertical projectors are drawn at the same scale. The difference is that while the plan is drawn at true scale, it is not true shape. Both receding lines are drawn at an angle of 30° either side of the perpendicular so the corners of the plan are represented by 120° or 60° instead of 90° as in planometric projection. All three surfaces can be equally scaled, but because of the distortion no orthographic plan or elevation can be used to form part of an isometric drawing.

PERSPECTIVE The projections so far described are without exception aerial views with parallel projectors and thus lack the natural form that would appeal to the ordinary observer.

Perspective pictorial projections, however, will produce a view which, because of the infinite choice of eye position and converging projectors, presents the three-dimensional almost as reality. There are three main categories, of which one-point (or parallel) and two-point (or angular) are the most common.

ONE-POINT In this projection a true-shape orthographic face (as with oblique cabinet projection) is used. All verticals remain vertical and one set of horizontals remains horizontal, while the other (receding) set converged on one vanishing point. It is without doubt the easiest of the perspectives to draw and is particularly useful in portraying interiors and giving 'depth' to sections. Many presentation section drawings adopt this projection to clarify form and composition.

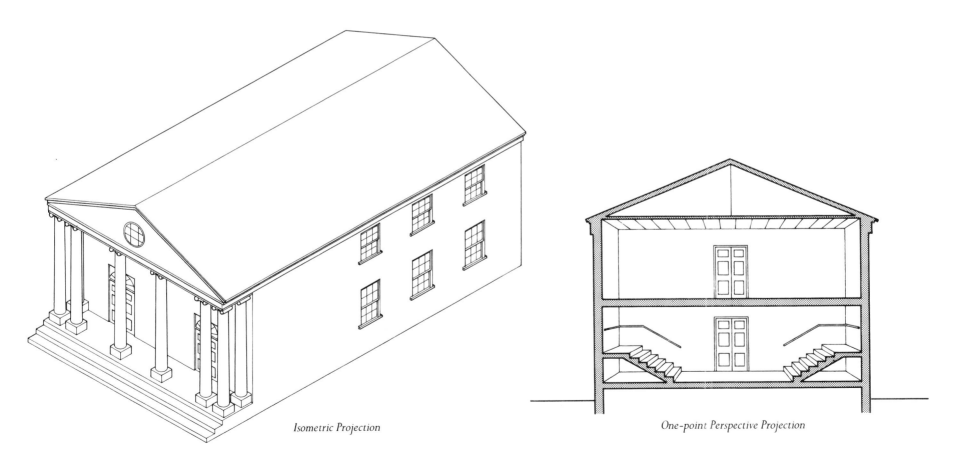

Isometric Projection

One-point Perspective Projection

TWO-POINT With this type, perhaps the most widely used, only the verticals remain undisturbed. Both sets of horizontals recede to their own vanishing points. It is not as straightforward to set up as one-point perspective, requiring a number of preliminary constructions before the actual drawing can be commenced. It is, however, extremely versatile, perhaps the most of all the projections, and can be readily adapted to meet most pictorial requirements. It still forms the basis of many three-dimensional presentation drawings.

Sciagraphy

Sciagraphy was originally the art of determining the time of day by the observation of shadows cast by a natural light source upon a dial. Nowadays the most common meaning is the projection of shadows upon two-dimensional or three-dimensional drawings. Elevations of any architectural form in pure line have the disadvantage of only showing the form as if the eye is opposite each part simultaneously, so that it appears 'flat' and thus unreal. The three-dimensional drawing in pure line, while giving an accurate picture of form and massing, remains equally unreal. In a world of light, change of tonal value is the basis of perception of form, and the addition of shade and shadow gives the illusion of solidity. With the expression of depth and the form of flat, curved or angled surfaces, the drawing becomes 'alive'.

While the artist is concerned with lighting from all directions, the architectural draughtsman requires fixed light from one direction only, in order that different forms and surfaces may be compared. The conventional direction of light has been fixed as the diagonal of a cube from the top left front corner to the bottom right rear corner. The illuminating rays are therefore 45° in plan and 45° in elevation. Shadows in plan are projected from bottom left to top right. Shadows in elevation are projected from top left to bottom right. It may be helpful in interpreting drawings with this treatment to remember that (i) the shade is the part of the form which is receiving no light; (ii) the shadow is the area behind the form obscuring the light (and is thus the silhouette of the form as projected by the light source).

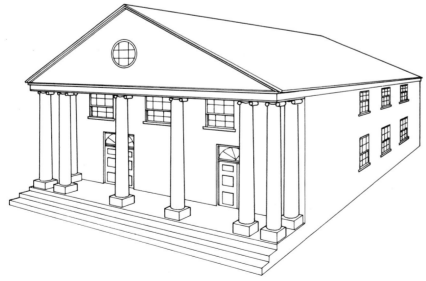

Two-point Perspective Projection

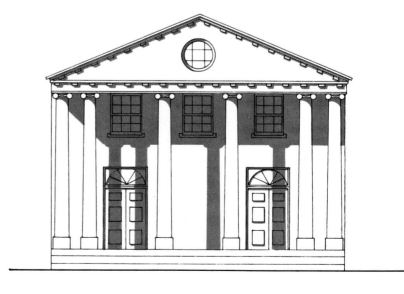

Sciagraphy

A NOTE ON
DRAWING MATERIALS
AND LETTERING

Drawing materials and styles of lettering have varied throughout history, and the development of the former has invariably influenced the latter, as has the changing purpose of the architectural drawing.

Drawing Materials

It is difficult to give any precise dates for the introduction of different drawing materials and instruments. The thirteenth-century tombstone of the architect Hugh Libergier at Rhiems shows a rule, square and compass – essential implements which must have been in use by masons since early times. The sketchbook of Villard d'Honnecourt is made of vellum (calf-skin) and the drawings are done in ink with a quill pen. The ink would probably have been made from carbon black, such as is produced by a smoking candle, mixed with water. The Renaissance period gradually saw the replacement of parchment and vellum by paper made from pulped rags, but this was still a precious commodity and only available in small sheets. It is much easier to use than vellum, however, and may have contributed to a looser style of drawing. The delicate techniques of silverpoint and leadpoint which were used for figure drawing were unsuitable for architectural work so ink,

or sepia from cuttlefish, was still the main medium. Most Renaissance drawings give the appearance of being freehand, although some sort of graduated scale must have been used even if the lines were not ruled. The value of paper meant that several different ideas were developed on one sheet, which might include figure studies, machinery and ornament as well as plans and views of buildings. The most famous examples of this range of interests are in the drawings of Leonardo da Vinci, but although his ideas are particularly remarkable, the drawings of his contemporaries give much the same effect. Like Villard d'Honnecourt, architects of the Renaissance would fill sketchbooks with designs and ornaments which might be useful at a later date. Often several pages would be filled with comparative studies of capitals of columns, mouldings or ornamental panels, and there might also be plans of a few buildings, real or projected.

With the change in attitude to drawing in the time of Antonio da Sangallo, the drawings became larger (having been not much more than quarto or foolscap before this time) and the use of elevations rather than sections with perspective interiors introduced a need for ruled lines drawn with a square. Washes were commonly introduced for shadows, but many of the drawings which survive still show that they were used for working out ideas, rather than for presenting a finished scheme. It was probably in this period that the T square, adjustable square and protractor came into use, the squares made then as now from hard wood, and the other instruments from brass. By the seventeenth century, the drawings of Borromini are built up on a grid of parallel lines which look as if a T square had been used. A plate in Andrea Pozzo's *Perspectiva Pictorum* shows a drawing table (with the board at what is surely an artificially steep angle) with two squares, a ruling pen with two metal points of adjustable width, and a quill for freehand drawing. There are also some dividers, and we may assume that compasses were in use too.

Buchotte's *Les Règles du Dessin et du Lavis* of 1722 gives the fullest written account up to this date of the materials and instruments used in drawing by architects and military engineers, and from what he writes one may suspect that it was French military engineers who introduced a number of conventions of drawing which had not previously concerned architects. Ten colours in common use are listed: *encre de la Chine* (of which the best actually came from China, then as now), *carmine, ultramarine* (lapis lazuli), *gamboge, verd de gris liquide* (presumably copper sulphate, used for water) *bistre* (dark brown made from the soot of a wood fire), *l'Inde fin* (indigo, used for colouring glass, iron and slates), two different sorts of green — *verd de vessie* and *verd d'iris,* and *vermillion* (mercuric oxide, used for colouring bricks and tiles). The powdered pigment was mixed by finger with water containing gum arabic in a little straight-sided white china pot. Quill pens were used for drawing lines, and graphite pencils from England were a new invention. Buchotte recommends that drawing instruments should be bought together in '*un étui de Mathématique*', containing a compass, an ebony rule, dividers, protractor and draughtsman's needle (for pricking through drawings). Small soft hair brushes would also be needed for washes. There were about ten different papers (identifiable by watermark) which could be relied upon. They were better if old, provided they had been kept in a dry place.

The draughtsman's equipment remained in this simple form for the rest of the eighteenth century. Joshua Kirby's *Perspective* (1754) includes a parallel rule among the instruments, a device made with two rules of equal size joined with metal pivots. He still recommended, however, that it should be used in conjunction with measurements made with dividers. Kirby also mentions the sector, a jointed scale used for dividing a line into any number of equal divisions, and for other calculations. Kirby also developed and published a grand folio volume on the 'Architectonic Sector' (1761), a device calibrated with the proportions of the five architectural Orders, which enabled their outlines to be drawn to any scale.

Around 1800 a considerable change occurred in the manufacture of paper with smooth 'wove' sheets taking the place of the earlier 'laid' paper with its prominent chain lines. The use of wood pulp as well as rag enabled much more paper to be produced, and mills producing rolls of paper were introduced, the size having previously been limited to the mould which could be lifted from the vat (Antiquarian, the largest size of hand-made paper, is 53 by 31 inches). As a result, architectural drawings of all kinds became larger, and more drawings were produced for each building. How much this was related to a breakdown in craftsmanship and the imposition of new styles, as has often been assumed, and how much to the new availability of paper, is difficult to tell. The introduction of tracing also caused a vast increase in the number of drawings produced, since duplicate sets of working drawings were needed for different contractors and for the office files. The task of tracing usually fell to the articled pupils in architects' offices, since it was not only monotonous, but it was thought that they would learn to design this way. Oiled linen was used for strength but it was a notoriously difficult material to draw on with a ruling pen, itself not an easy instrument to use. Linen was replaced by tracing paper in most offices after the First World War. For presentation drawings Whatman paper was usually preferred on both sides of the Atlantic. The watermark gives the year of production, although it can only serve as a *terminus ante quem* when dating drawings. For perspectives and other wash drawings the paper would be stretched by wetting with a sponge and pasting down the edges on to a sheet of stiff cardboard. During the 1920s gouache was preferred to transparent watercolour for perspectives. Otherwise there were few changes in the basic materials in use until the introduction of German stylographic pens, with their even mechanical line, and what might be described as the 'Letraset revolution' of the 1960s. The latter introduced rub-down lettering, symbols, cars, trees and people; it led to a uniformity in the presentation style of architects' drawings and a sad decline in traditional draughting skills. For reproducing drawings in the office, tracing had been replaced by the 'blueprint' copying process in around 1900. This produced a white-line image on a blue background. This, in turn, was superseded by the dye-line process which has been used since the 1920s.

Lettering

With the relatively informal use of architectural drawings before the nineteenth century, lettering played a small part in the presentation of a scheme, being usually done in copper-plate hand. In the post-Waterloo period in England it was common to imitate the austere 'grotesque' of *sans serif* printing types of the time, occasionally enlivened by the use of shadowed faces. These were parodied by Pugin for their meanness of effect, and he often used black letters, which became naturally associated with the Gothic Revival. From this point, the lettering on English drawings follows closely the progress of styles and the use of fantastic and invented letter forms based on Romanesque uncials. It began with William Burges in the 1850s. In Norman Shaw's lettering, as in his architecture, there is a gradual return to classical ortho-doxy, although he enjoyed certain characteristic distortions of letter forms which were widely copied and, in exaggerated form, provided the basis of the eccentric lettering styles of Voysey, Mackintosh and their Continental imitators. It was often remarked in the 1890s that the lettering on drawings was made purposely illegible, but before the First World War the influence of Edward Johnston and Eric Gill (who turned to lettering from being a pupil in the office of W D Caroë), together with a renewed interest in Classicism, brought about a uniformity of style based on the lettering on the base of Trajan's Column in Rome. This had already become a standard for the much more Classically conscious Americans.

The introduction of packing-case style stencil lettering by Le Corbusier in the 1920s was highly influential. It was probably based originally on the use of such lettering in Cubist paintings by Picasso and Braque, where it represented a sort of non-associational *objet-type* like the pipe or the playing card. It had the advantage of being quicker and easier than traditional drawn lettering, as well as giving an immediately identifiable 'modern' look to drawings on which it was used. In some cases it has even survived the onslaught of rub-down instant lettering.

BIBLIOGRAPHY

Ackerman, James S, 'Architectural Practice in the Italian Renaissance', in *Renaissance Art,* C. Gilbert (ed.), London: Harper & Row, 1970

Blomfield, Reginald, *Architectural Drawing and Draughtsmen,* London: Cassell & Co., 1912

Blunt, A, *Art and Architecture in France 1500-1700,* London: Penguin Books, 1953

Bowie, Theodore (ed.), *The Sketchbook of Villard de Honnecourt,* Bloomington and London: Indiana University Press, 1959

Braham, Allan, *The Architecture of the French Enlightenment,* London: Thames & Hudson, 1980

Brown University, *Ornament and Architecture: Renaissance Drawings, Prints and Books,* Rhode Island: Thames & Hudson, 1980

Bruschi, Arnaldo, *Bramante,* London: Thames & Hudson, 1977

Bucher, François, *Architector: The Lodgebooks and Sketchbooks of Medieval Masons,* 4 vols. New York: Abaris Books, 1979

Cable, Carole, *The Architectural Drawing: its development and history 1300-1950.* Monticello, Illinois: Vance bibliographies, 1978

Cinque Secoli di Architettura nel Disegno Dell'Edificio e Dell' Ornamento, Milano:Stampa della stanza del Borgo, 1975

Collins, George R, *Visionary Drawings of Architecture and Planning, 20th Century through the 1960s,* Cambridge, Mass.: MIT Press, 1979

Coulin, Claudius, *Drawings by Architects from the Ninth Century to the Present Day,* New York: Reinhold, 1962

Dessins Anciens D'Architecture et de Décoration, (Anne de Herdt), Geneva: Musée d'Art et D'Histoire, Cabinet des Dessins, 1979

Dilke, Lady Emilia Frances Strong, *French Engravers and Draughtsmen in the Eighteenth Century,* London: George Bell & Sons, 1902

Drexler, Arthur, *The Drawings of Frank Lloyd Wright,* London: Thames & Hudson, 1970.

Drexler, Arthur (ed.), *The Architecture of the École des Beaux-Arts,* New York: Museum of Modern Art, 1977

Descargues, Pierre, *Perspective,* New York: Harry N Abrams, Inc., 1977

Edgerton, Samuel Y Jr, *The Renaissance Rediscovery of Linear Perspective,* London: Harper & Row, 1967

Fiske Kimball, *The Creation of the Rococo Decorative Style,* New York: Dover Publications, 1980

Fünf Architetten ans Fünf Jahrhunderten, (Ekhart Berkenhagen), Berlin: Kunstbibliothek Berlin, II, 1976.

Gebhard, David and Nevins, Deborah, *200 Years of Architectural Drawing,* New York: Watson-Guptill Publications, 1977.

Hall, Helen B (ed.) *Architectural and Ornament Drawings of the 16th to the early 19th centuries in the collection of the University of Michigan Museum of Art,* Michigan: University of Michigan, 1965.

Harris, John, *A Catalogue of British Drawings for Architecture, Decoration,*

Sculpture and Landscape Gardening 1550-1900 in American collections, London: Gregg Press, 1971.

Harris, John, Orgel, Stephen, and Strong, Roy, *The King's Arcadia; Inigo Jones and the Stuart Court,* London: Arts Council, 1973

Harris, John, and Tait, A A, *Catalogue of the Drawings by Inigo Jones, John Webb and Isaac de Caus at Worcester College,* Oxford: Clarendon Press, 1979

Hemple, Eberhard, *Baroque Art and Architecture in Central Europe,* London: Pelican Books, 1965

Huelsen, Christian, *Il Libro di Giuliano da Sangallo,* Leipzig: Cod. Vat. Barb. Cat. 4424, Codices Vaticani selecti, 1910.

Idee und Anspruch der Architecktur. Zeichnungen des 16. bis 20. Jahrhunderts ans dem Cooper Hewitt Museum, New York. Koln: Museum der Stadt Koln, 1979.

Ivins, W M Jr, *Prints and Visual Communications,* London: Routledge & Kegan Paul, 1953

Kauffman, Thomas Da Costa, 'The Perspective of Shadows', *Journal of the Warburg and Courtauld Institutes,* 38, (1975), pp. 258-271.

Kemper, Alfred M. *Drawings by American Architects,* New York: John Wiley & Sons, 1973

King, Susan, *The Drawings of Eric Mendelsohn,* Berkeley: University of California, 1969

Kitao, T K, 'Prejudice in Perspective: A Study of Vignola's Perspective Treatise', *Art Bulletin,* 44, (1962): pp. 173-94

Le Corbusier, *Le Corbusier Sketchbooks.* Notes by F. de Franclieu, Vols. 2 & 3 forthcoming, London: Thames & Hudson, 1981

Lewis, Douglas, *The Drawings of Andrea Palladio,* Washington: International Exhibitions Foundation, 1981.

Lever, Jill (ed.), *RIBA Drawings Catalogue,* Alphabetical series, Farnborough: 1968

Lotz, Wolfgang, *Studies in Italian Renaissance Architecture,* London: MIT Press, 1981.

Marconi P, Cipriani A, Valeriani E, *I disegni di architettura dell'Archivo storico dell Accademia di San Luca,* 2 vols, Rome: MIT Press, 1974

Nevins, Deborah, & Stern, Robert, *The Architect's Eye, American Architectural Drawings from 1799-1978,* New York: Pantheon Press, 1979

Nichols, Frederick Doveton, *Thomas Jefferson's Architectural Drawings,* Boston: Massachusetts Historical Society, 1969

Nicoll, Allardyce, *The Development of the Theatre,* London: George G Harrap & Co., 1927

Oncken, Alste, *Friedrich Gilly, 1772-1800,* Berlin: 1935

Physick, John, and Darby, Michael, *Marble Halls: Drawings and Models for Victorian Secular Buildings,* London: Thanet Press, 1973

Piranesi, G B, *Piranesi et les Français, 1740-1790,* Rome: Edizioni dell'Elefante, 1976

Portoghesi P, *Borromini nella cultura Europea,* Rome: Officina Edizioni, 1964

Plan und Bauwerk, Entwürfe aus fünf jahrhunderten, Bayerische Akademie der Schönen Kunste, 1952

RIBA Drawing Series, 1968, includes original architectural designs, sketches and perspectives covering five centuries, from the RIBA library. Each volume includes an introduction to the subject and a further reading list. Series published from 1968 onwards.

Rosenberg, J and Slive, S *Dutch Art and Architecture, 1600-1800,* London: Penguin Books, 1966.

Shelby, I R, *Gothic Design Techniques,* London: Southern Illinois University Press, 1977

Smithsonian Institution, *Crosscurrents, French and Italian Neoclassical Drawings and Prints . . .,* Washington DC: Smithsonian Institution Press, 1978

Stamp, Gavin, *The Great Perspectivists, RIBA Drawing Series,* London: Trefoil Books, 1982

Stampfle, Felice, *Giovanni Battista Piranesi: Drawings in the Pierpont Morgan Library,* New York: Dover Publications, 1978

Tendenzen der Zwanziger Jahre, N. 15. Berlin: Europäische Kunstausstellung, 1977

Thomas, Hylton, *The Drawings of Giovanni Battista Piranesi,* London: Faber & Faber, 1981

Von Schinkel bis Mies van der Rohe, Zeichneirische Entwürfe europäischer Baumeister, Raum-und Formgestalter 1789-1969, Berlin: Kunstbibliothek, 1974

Wittkower, Rudolf, and Brauer, Heinrich, *Die Zeichnungen des Gianlorenzo Bernini,* Berlin: 1931 (reprinted New York: Collectors Editions, 1970).

ACKNOWLEDGMENTS

Photographs were supplied by the museums, galleries and collections to which the drawings belong, with the exception of the following: Architectural Association 174, 175; Architectural Press 94-5; Archivio IGDA 70; Bullox 108-9; Courtauld Institute of Art 78, 85; Arthur Drexler, New York 157; Kustannusosakeyhtio Otava, Helsinki 166; Ivan Margolius: *Cubism In Architecture and The Applied Arts* (David & Charles, Newton Abbot, 1979) 150; Museum of Modern Art, New York 139; Richard Oliver, New York 54; Royal Commission On The Ancient and Historical Monuments of Scotland 96t; Alison Sky, New York 148-9.

The drawings in 'The History of Architectural Drawing' are reproduced by kind permission of: Bibliothèque Nationale, Paris 33, 39; Bodleian Library, Oxford 30b; Cranbrook Academy of Art Museum, Michigan, Illinois 59; École Nationale Supérieure des Beaux-Arts, Paris 42; Hunterian Museum, The Mackintosh Collection, University of Glasgow 50; Allen Lane (*Borromini,* Anthony Blunt, 1979) 26; Library of St Gallen, Switzerland 13; Metropolitan Museum of Art, New York 20; Museum Der Bildenden Künste, Leipzig 25; National Gallery of Scotland, Edinburgh 35; RIBA 24, 28, 30t, 34, 43, 45, 46, 52, 56, 57, 58; John Rivers Collection, Houston, Texas 54; Staatliche Museen, Berlin 41; James Stirling 60; Uffizi Gallery, Florence 18, 19; Victoria & Albert Museum 22, 31, 36, 47, 49.

The drawings on pages 160 and 161 are © by SPADEM, Paris 1982.

INDEX

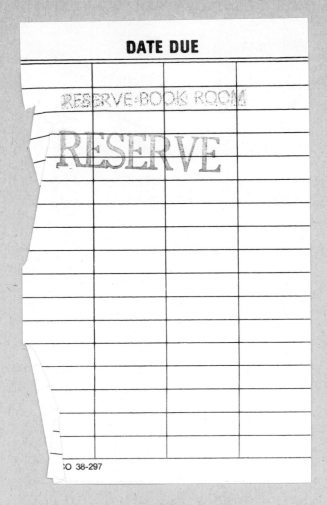